Dancing on Rainbows

Dancing on Rainbows

A Celebration of Numismatic Art

Roy G. Biv

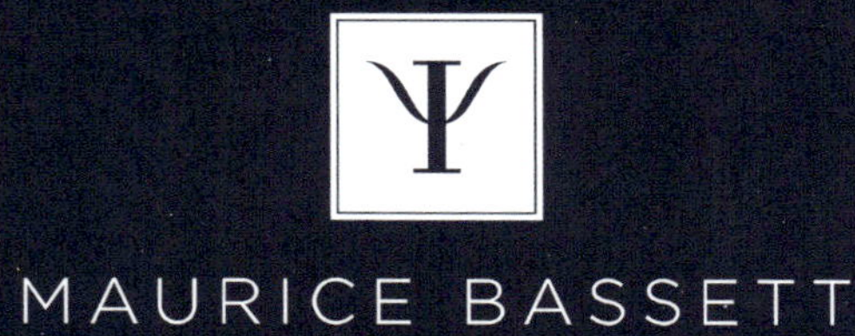

Maurice Bassett

Dancing on Rainbows: A Celebration of Numismatic Art

Numismatic Art Series #1

Maurice Bassett
P.O. Box 839
Anna Maria, FL 34216-0839

MauriceBassett@gmail.com
www.MauriceBassett.com

For information about bulk order discounts for businesses and organizations, please contact the publisher at MauriceBassett@gmail.com

Photography by BluCC Photos
www.bluccphotos.com

Cover design by David Michael Moore

Layout by Chris Nelson

ISBN: 978-1-60025-159-7

CONTENTS

INTRODUCTION

Coin collectors have collected toned coins for years, but the popularity of rainbow-toned coins is a relatively recent phenomenon. This book is a carefully curated sampling of some of the finest rainbow-toned coins that have come on the market in recent years.

Glowing neon colors; "Lucky Charms" colors; peacock colors; pastel colors; thick, "heavy" colors; banded rainbow colors; crescent-shaped, double crescent-shaped and arch-shaped colors and more . . . All are gathered together here for your enjoyment. While these coins are each one-of-a-kind due to their unique toning, what they do have in common, with only a few exceptions, is that they are all either rainbow-toned or "monster"-toned U.S. coins. To me, these naturally toned coins are works of art—nature's art.

In assembling this collection, I've aimed to create something special that would give the same sense of exhilaration and delight a child gets experiencing fireflies in the garden or in the woods at night. The same "wow" produced by a beautiful butterfly or a gorgeous sunrise or sunset. The same joy produced by, yes, rainbows big and small.

Rainbows are joygiving, and, to me, quite literally a gift from God. And we are surrounded by rainbows, though most of us don't even know it . . . If you hold a prism up to a light source you'll see how light consists of a spectrum of colors. You can't actually see light itself—only its reflection off objects in the environment—but you can enjoy seeing the reflected colors and also, via the prism, the colors that make up the light itself.

It's common to see rainbows during a rain shower—hence the name "rainbow"—and you can create your own rainbows any time you like by taking a hose and spraying water up in the air on a sunny day. The truth is you aren't actually creating rainbows with your spray of water, as it may appear at first. Rather, you're revealing what's already there. The light all around you is already made up of rainbow colors, whether you see them or not. The water and the prism simply reveal them.

Think about it. Whether you're conscious of it or not, we live surrounded by rainbows and latent rainbows, surrounded by beauty and latent beauty. And we can tap into that beauty any time we like simply by remembering it's there. When you remember, you keep your sense of meaning alive. You keep the child within you alive. The magic alive. You unify your divisions.

So I invite you to turn the page and begin to dance on rainbows along with me now, one coin at a time. May you find them to be joygiving and may they also give you a fresh, new appreciation for nature's art. Perhaps the images will even inspire you to start your own collection of rainbow-toned coins, or find new ones to add to your existing collection.

Roy G. Biv

Dancing on Rainbows

Chapter 1

Morgan Dollars - Obverse Toned

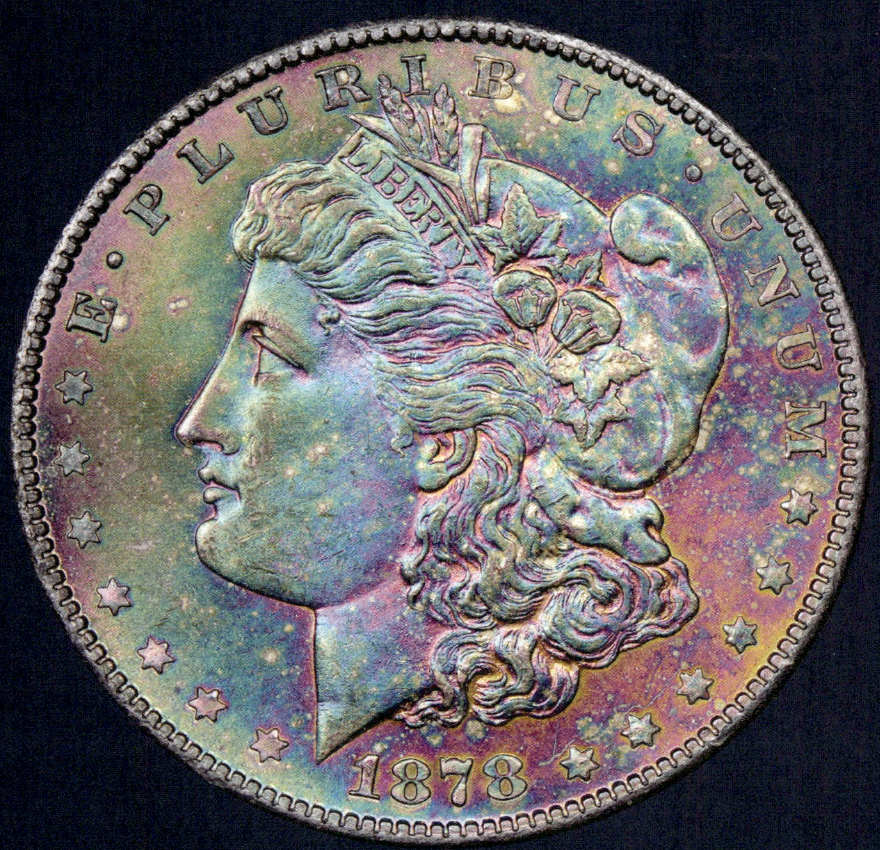

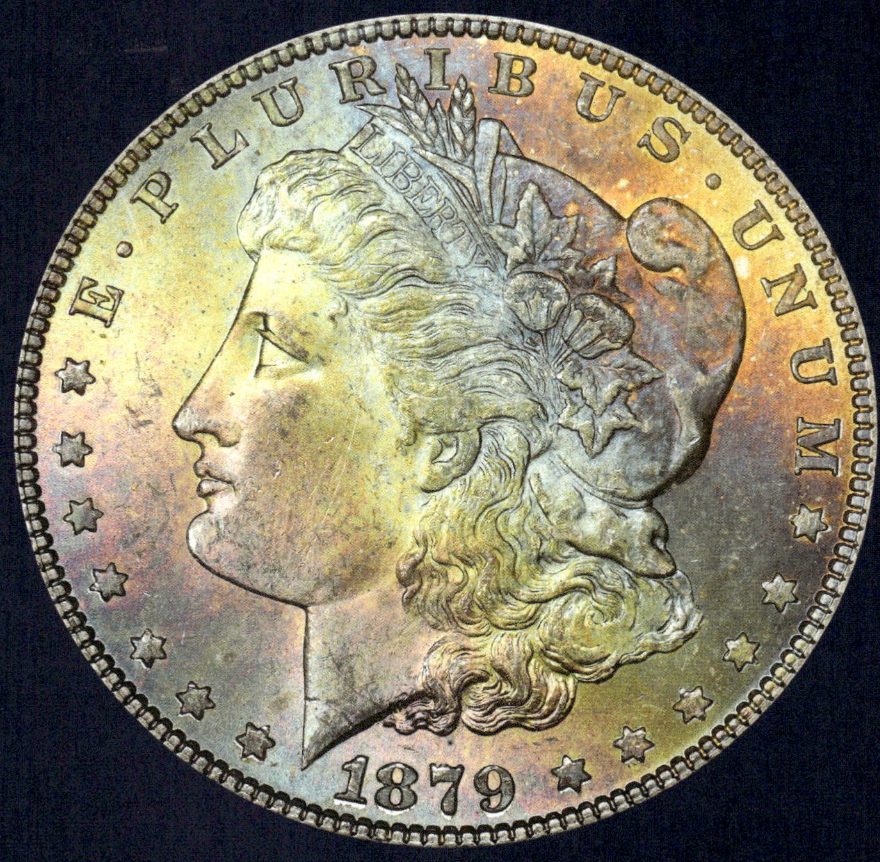

"The Nebula"
1878-S $1 NGC MS64★
Certification number 2083152-035
Ex. "Col." E.H.R. Green
Ex. Eric P. Newman Collection

1879 $1 PCGS MS63
Certification number 18131641

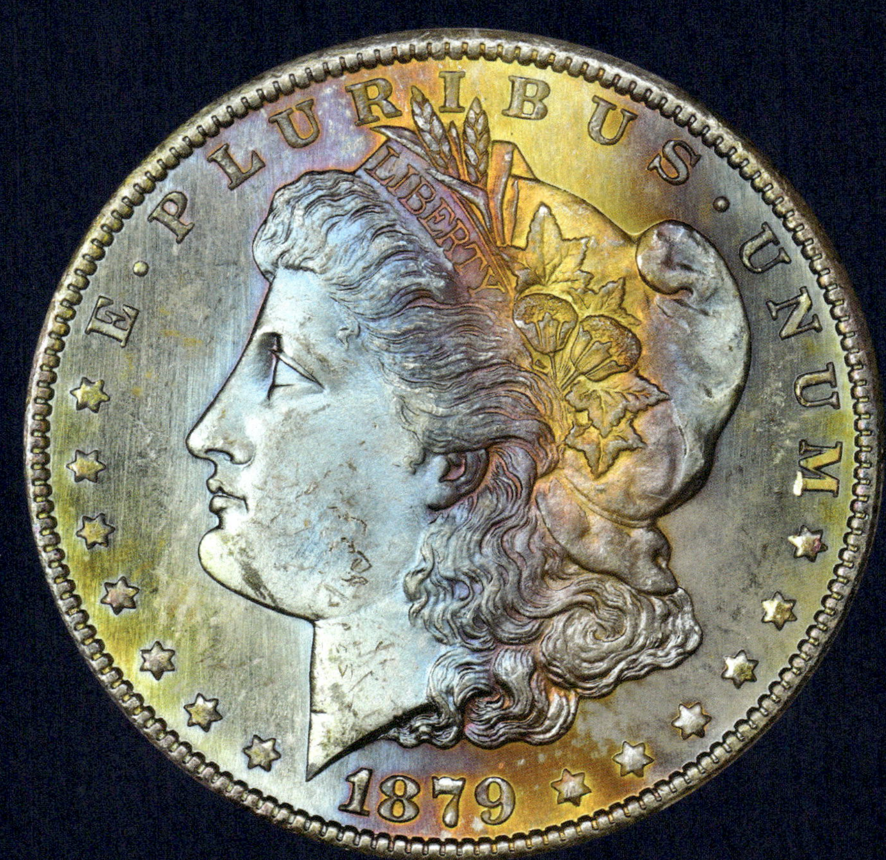

"Avatar"
1879-S $1 PCGS MS63
Certification number 33490613

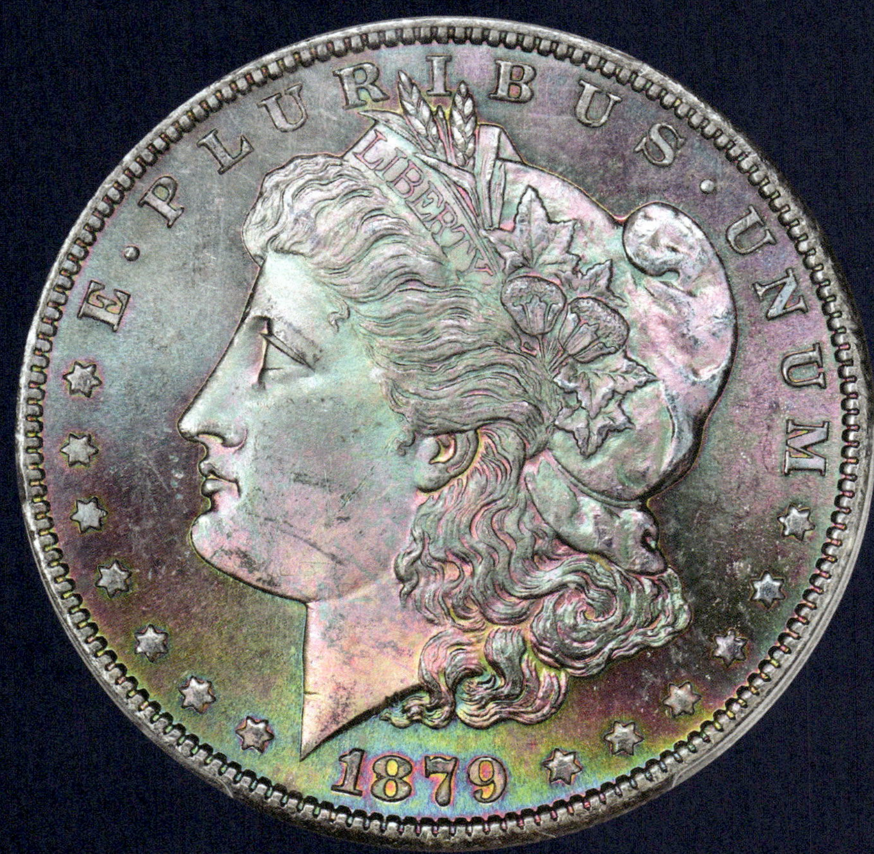

"Purple Sunset"
1879-S $1 PCGS MS66
Certification number 81816431

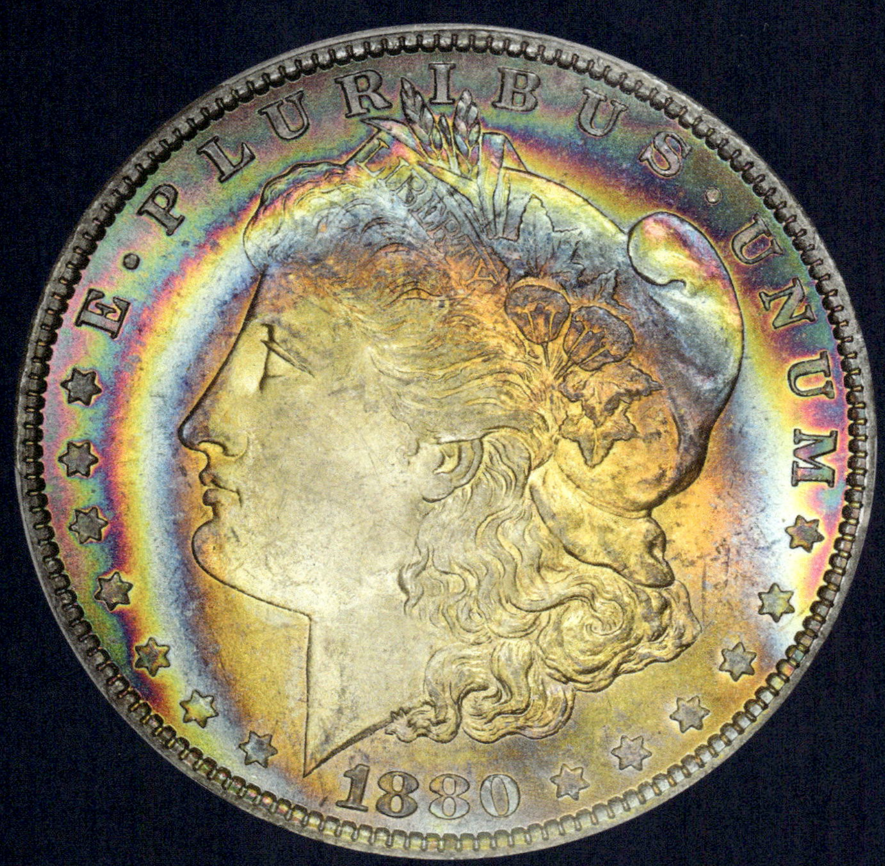

“Rainbow Arch”
1880-O $1 PCGS MS64
Certification number 84298672

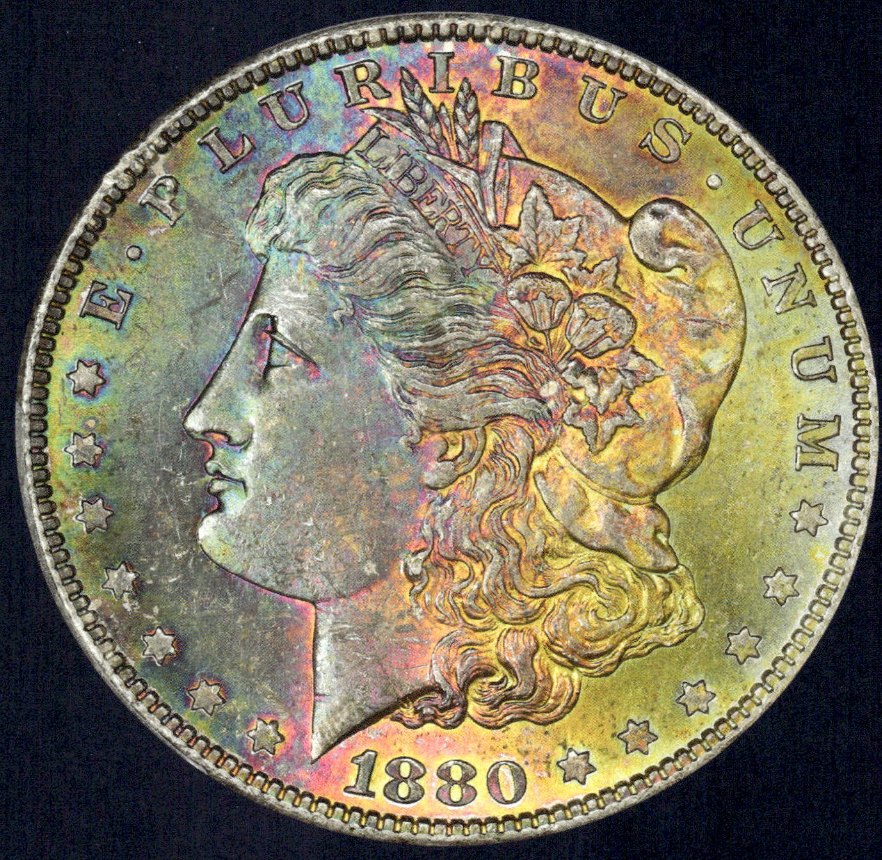

1880-S $1 PCGS MS65
Certification number 33197181

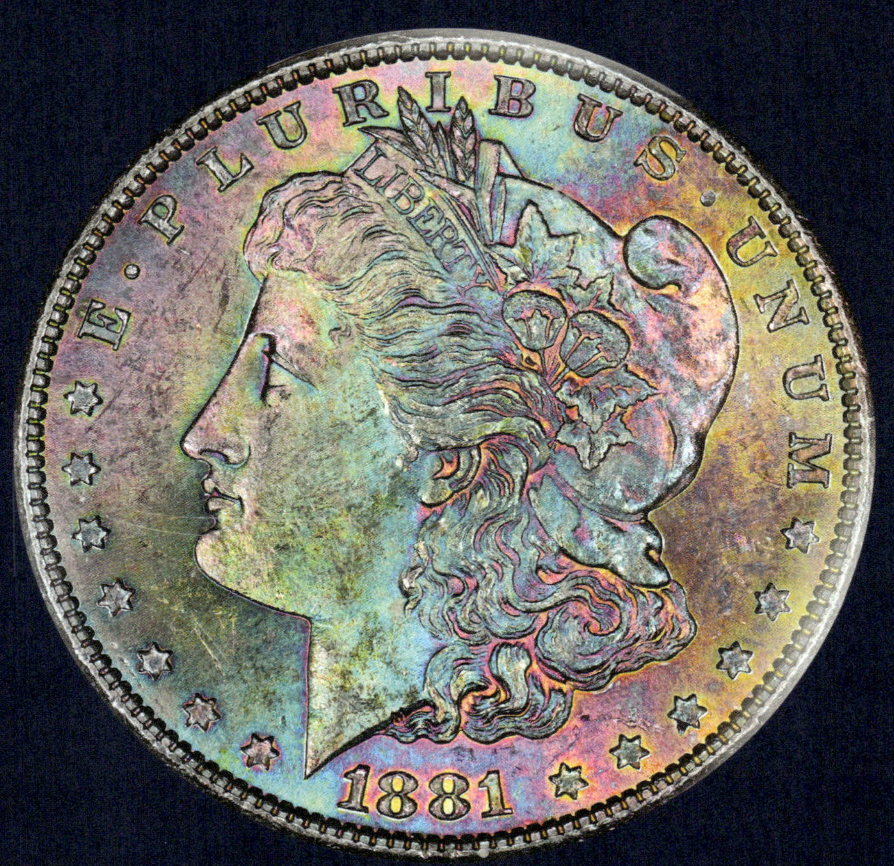

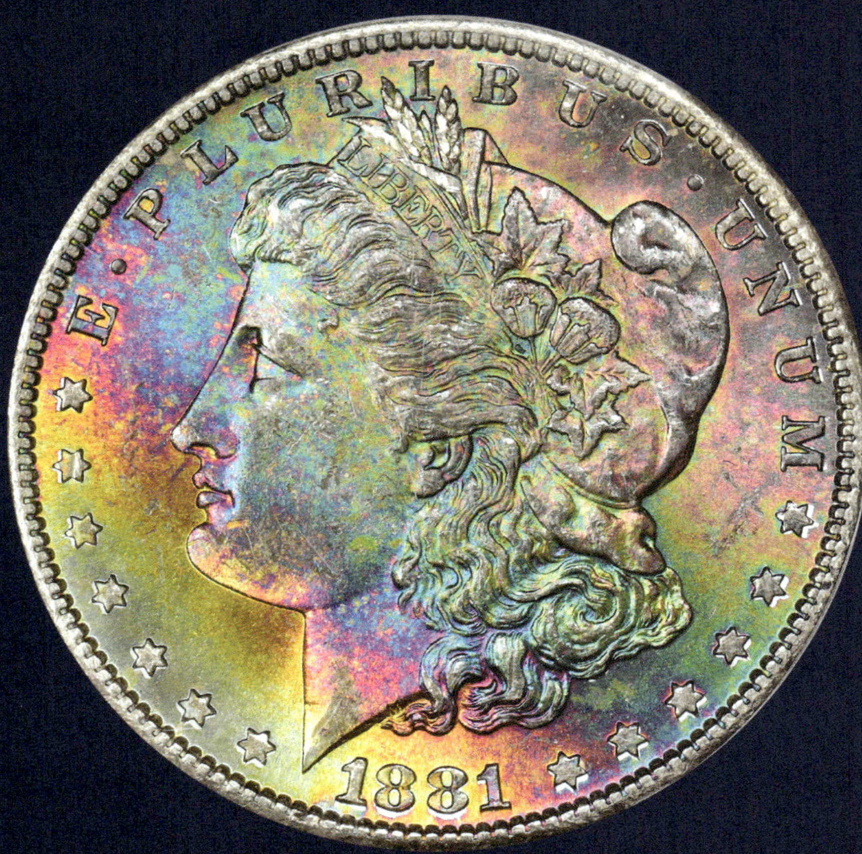

1881-S $1 PCGS MS64
Certification number 84102999

1881-S $1 PCGS MS65+
Certification number 84701226

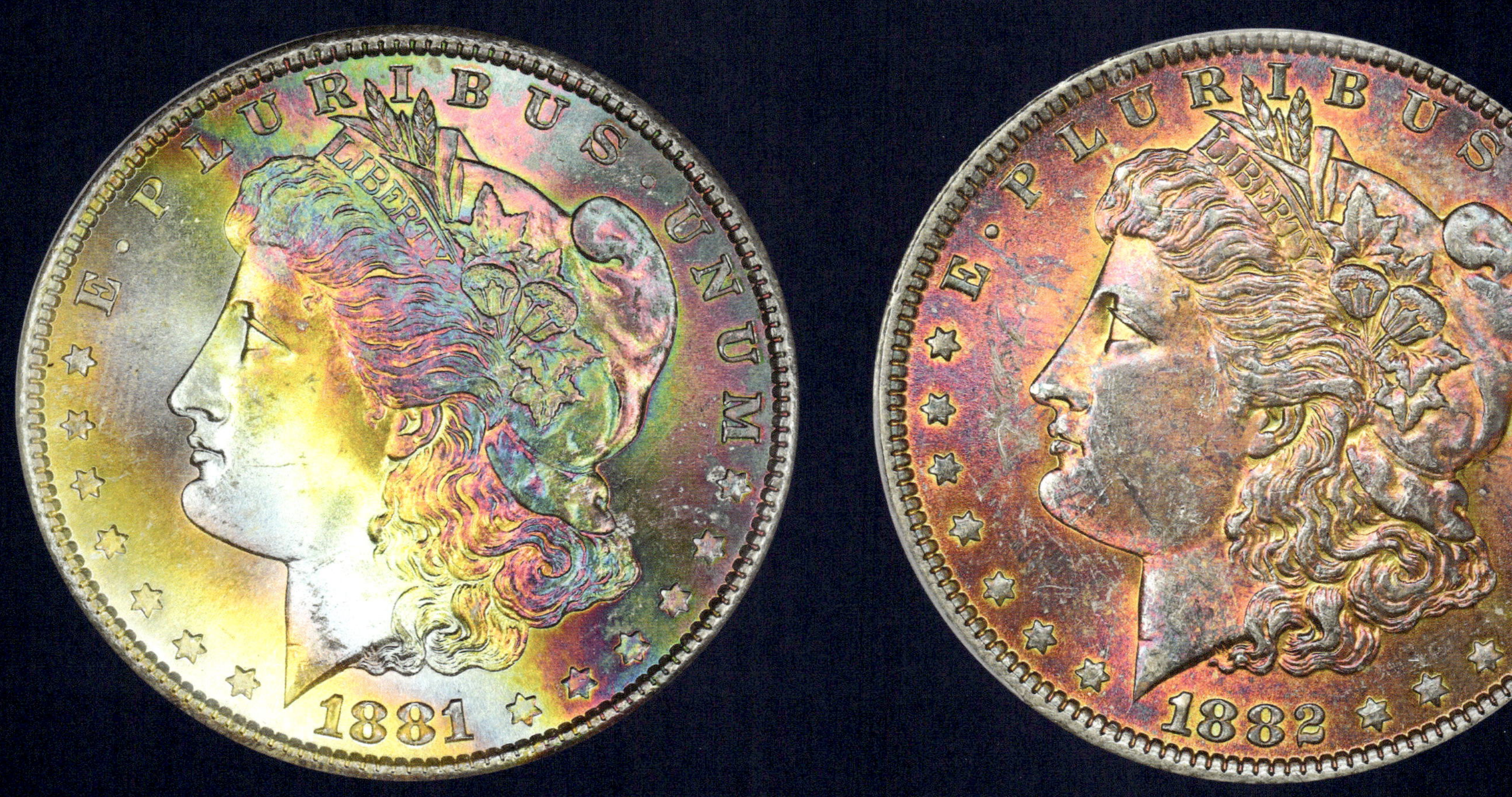

1881-S $1 PCGS MS66
Certification number 90077843

"The Fireball"
1882-O $1 PCGS MS63
Certification number 37746272

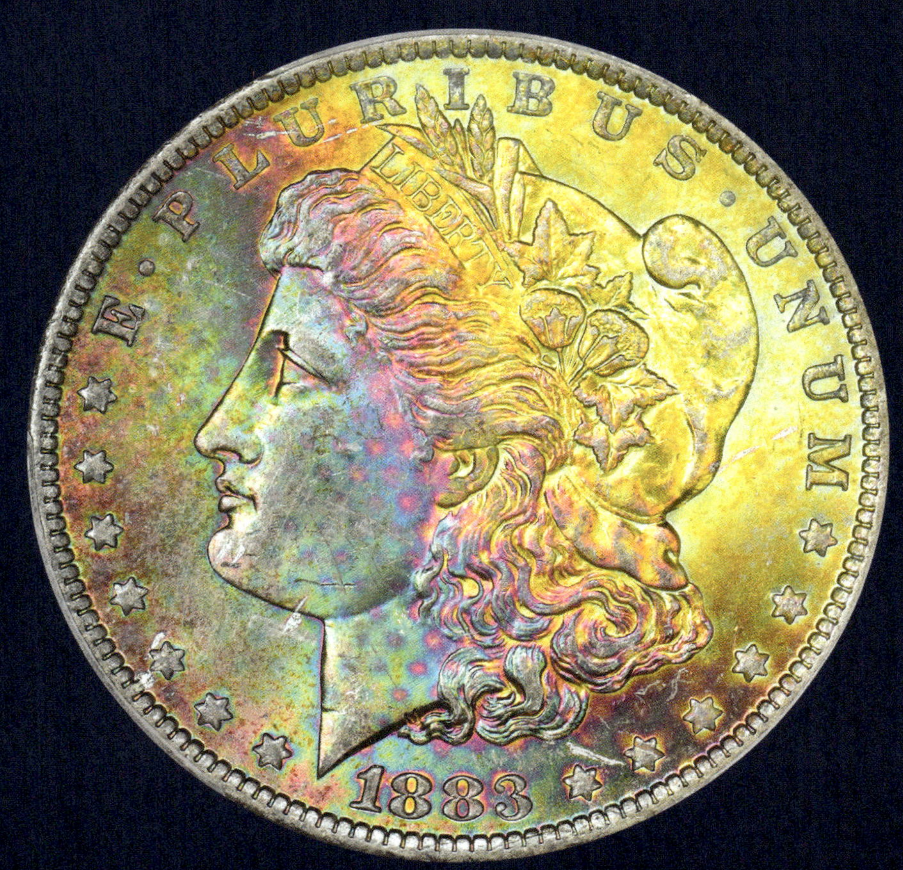

1883-O $1 PCGS MS63
Certification number 38410927

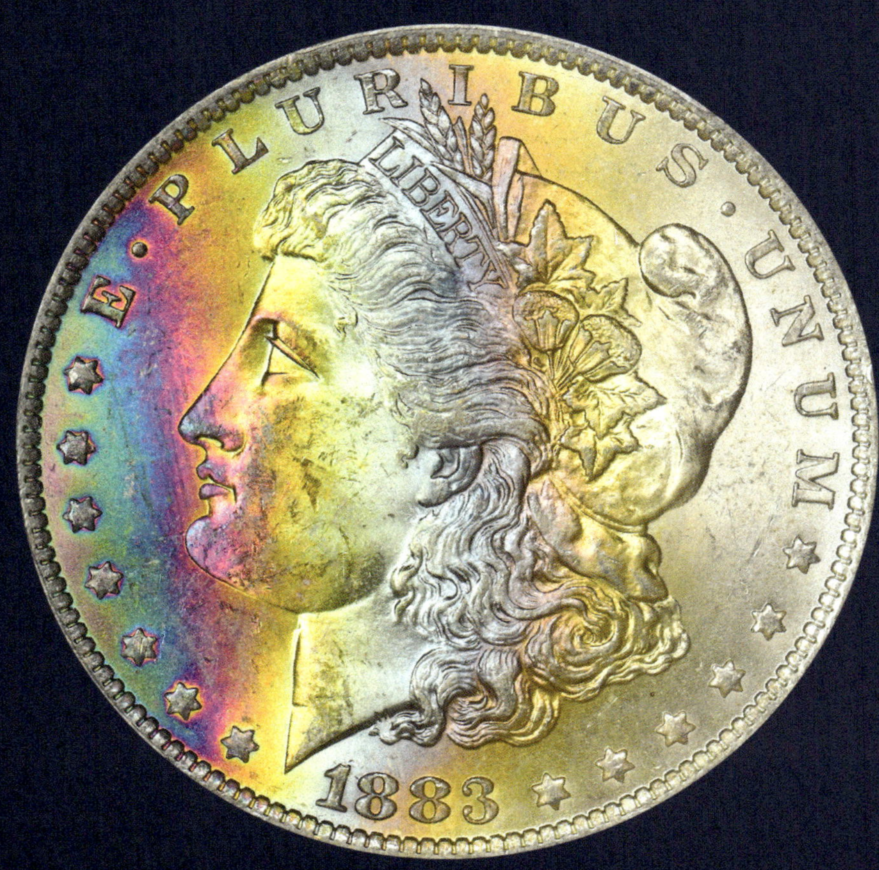

1883-O $1 PCGS MS64
Certification number 81706522

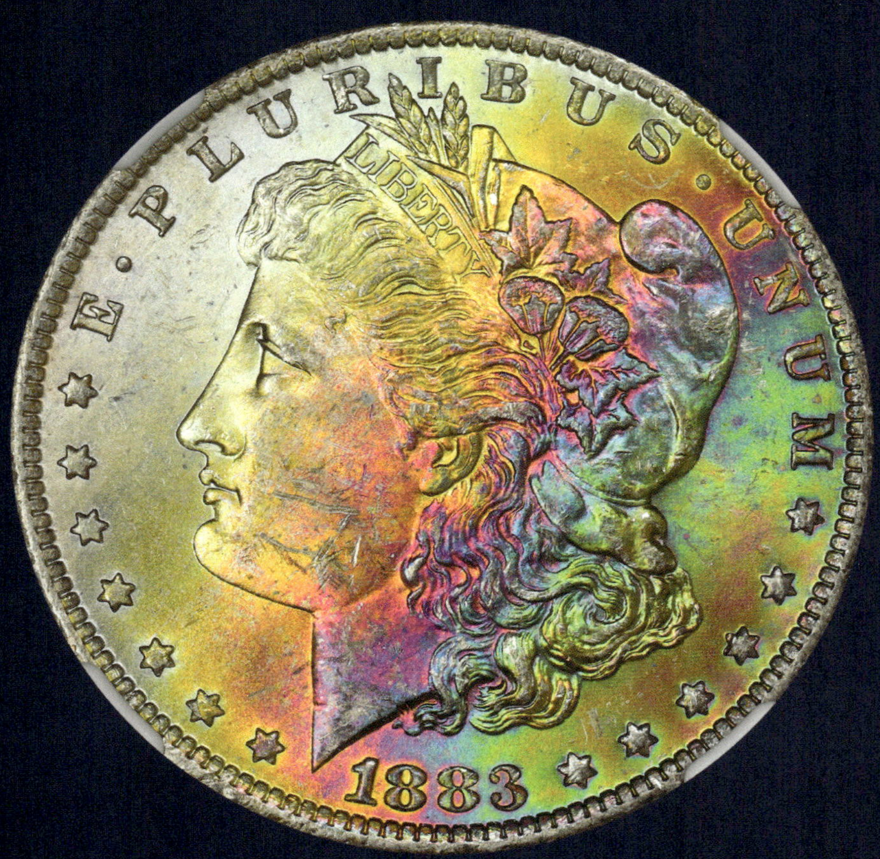

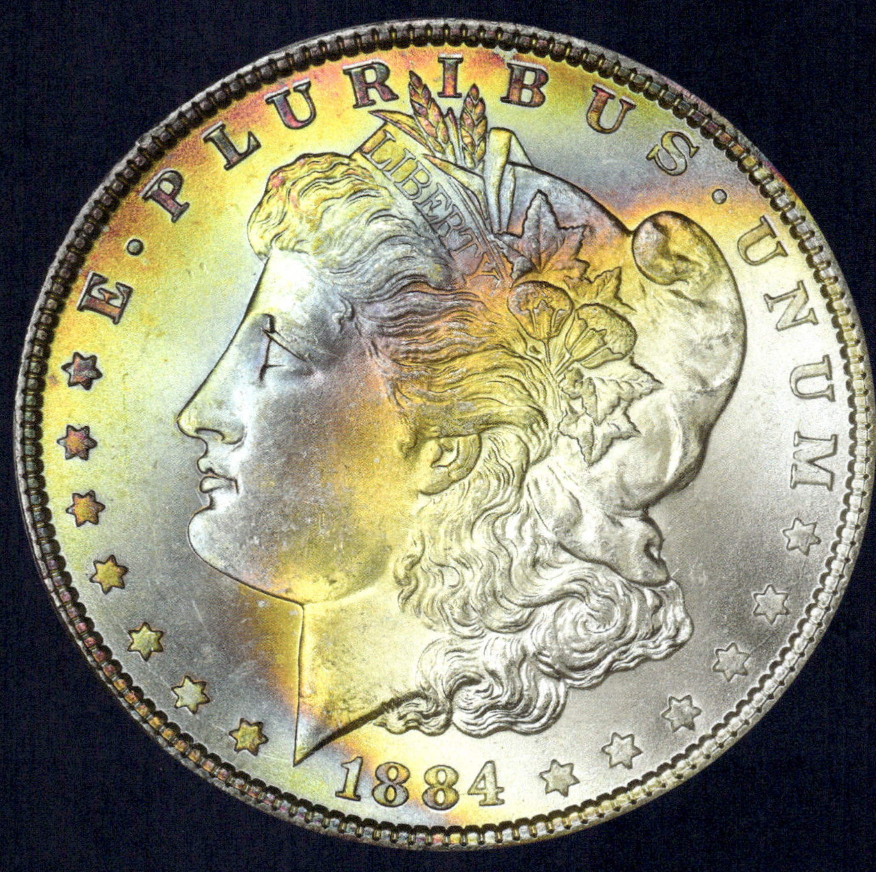

1883-O $1 NGC MS64★
Certification number 4525408-001

1884 $1 PCGS MS65
Certification number 83661295

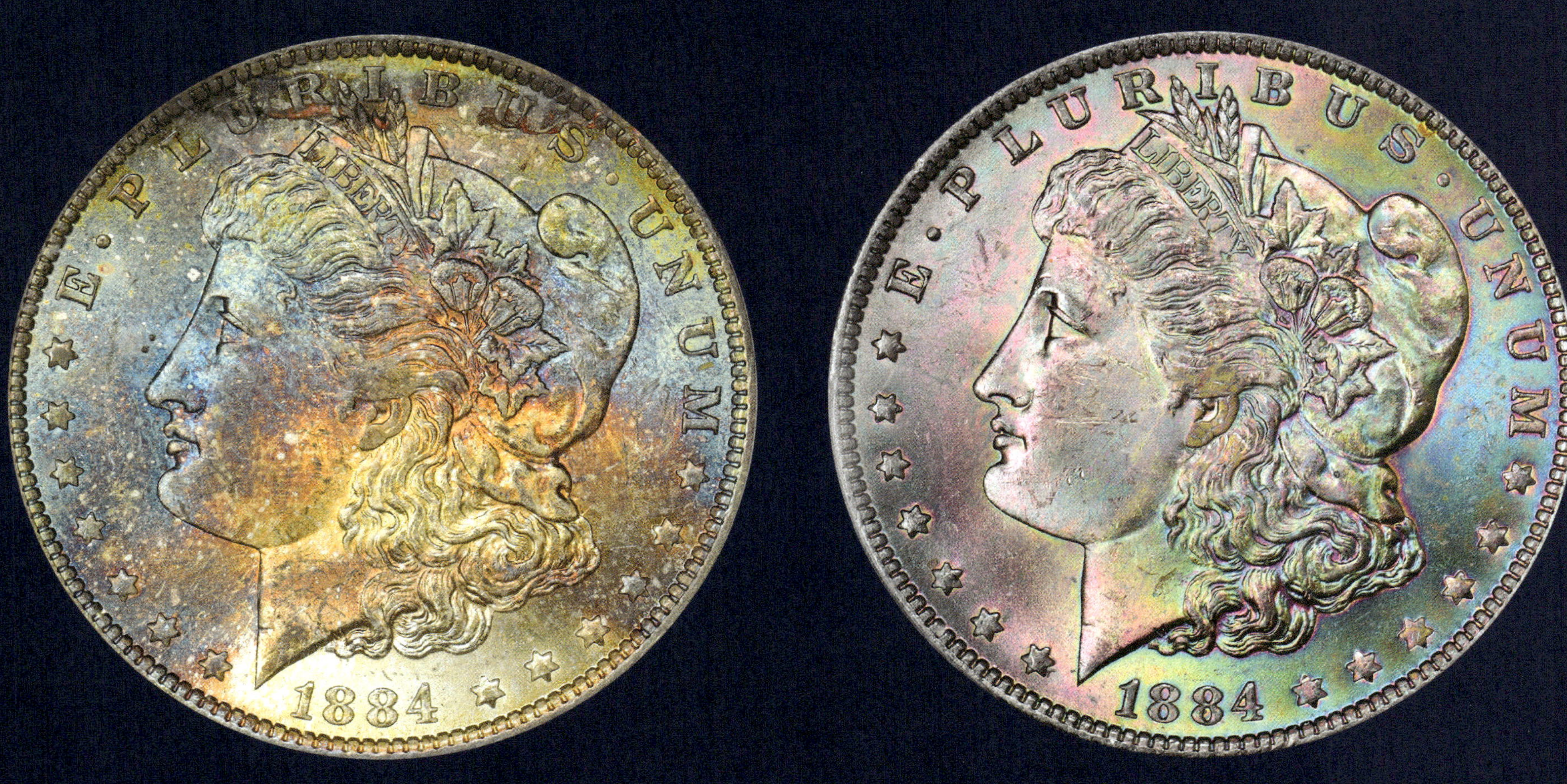

"Stardust"
1884-O $1 PCGS MS64
Certification number 7827719

1884-O $1 PCGS MS64
Certification number 27777129

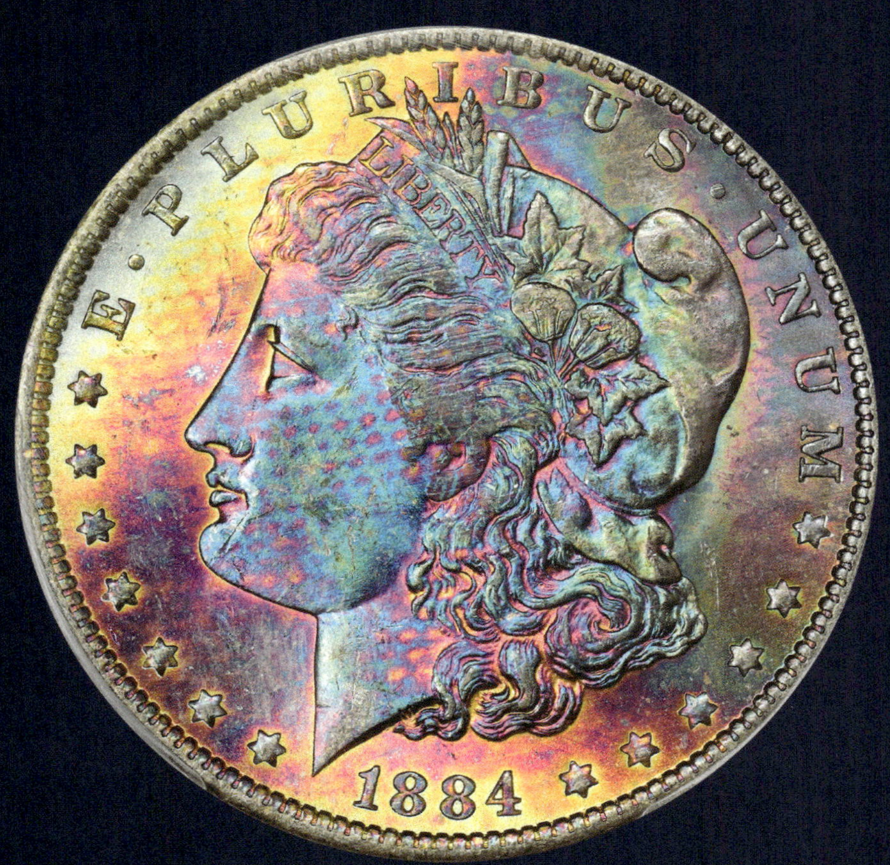

1884-O $1 PCGS MS64
Certification number 36385360

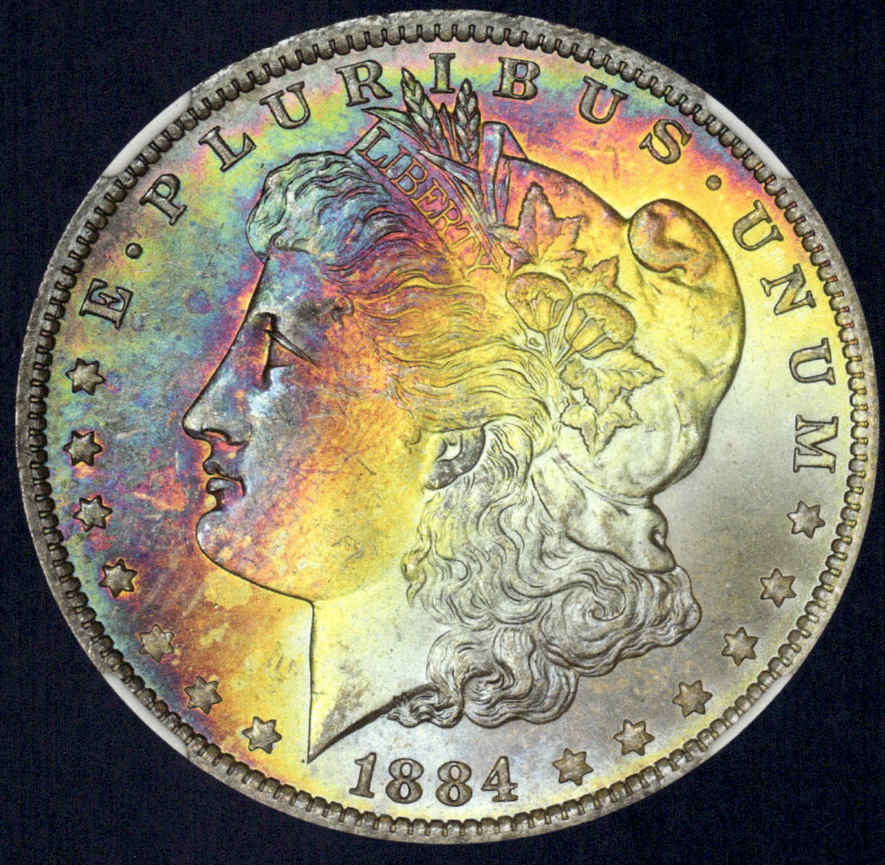

1884-O $1 NGC MS66★
Certification number 4669055-006

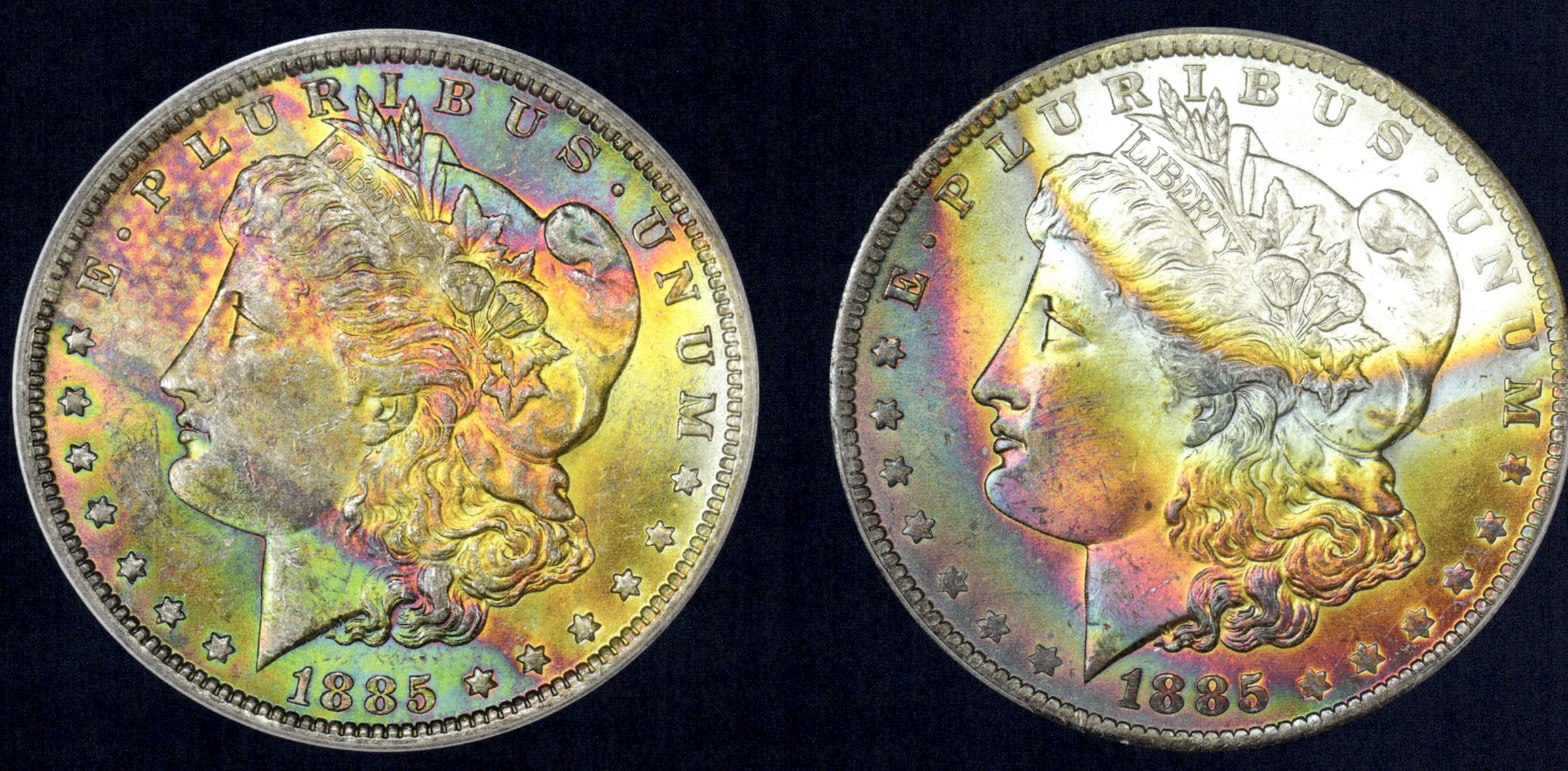

1885-O $1 PCGS MS63
Certification number 14086126

1885-O $1 PCGS MS64
Certification number 84201268

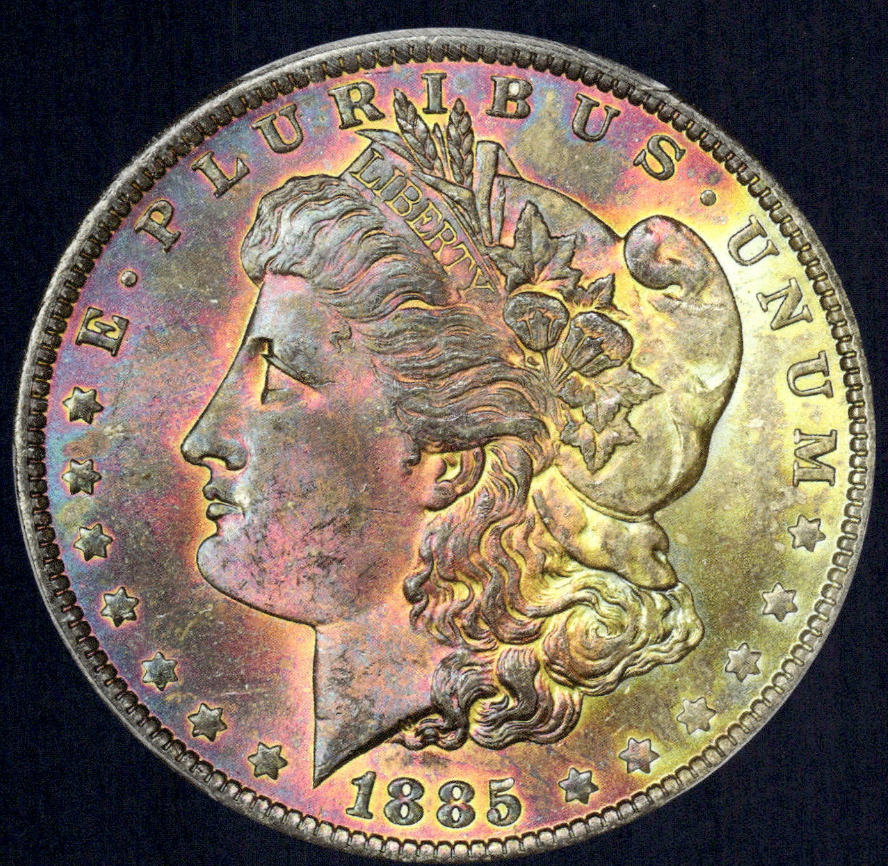

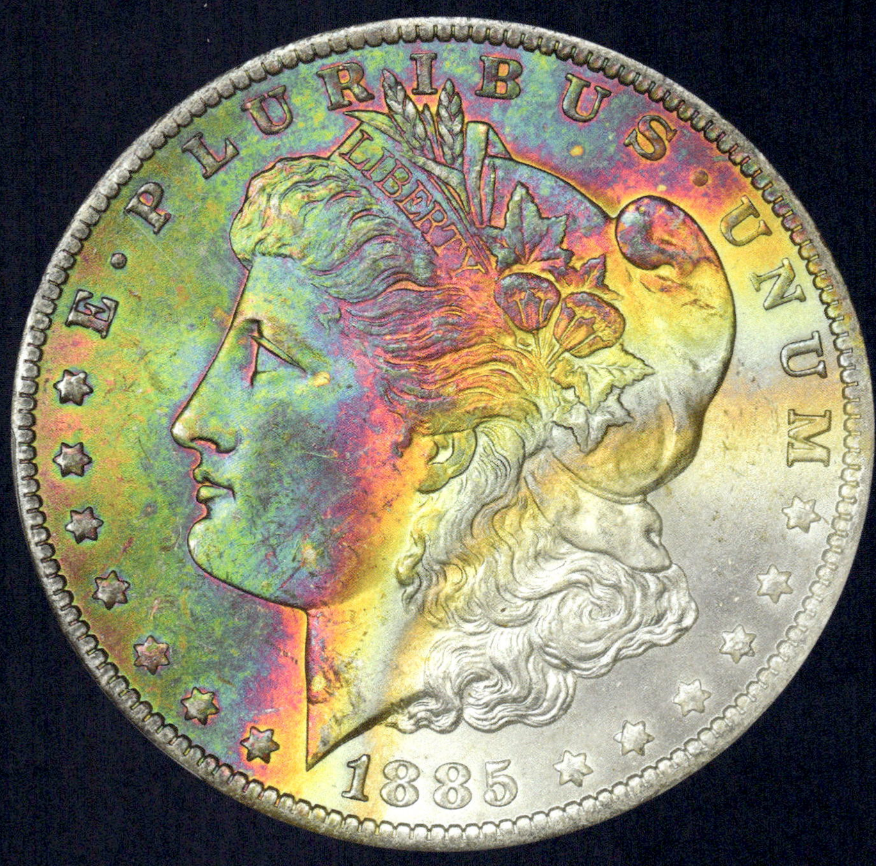

1885-O $1 PCGS MS65
Certification number 84201254

"Irish Rainbow"
1885-O $1 PCGS MS66+
Certification number 36857503

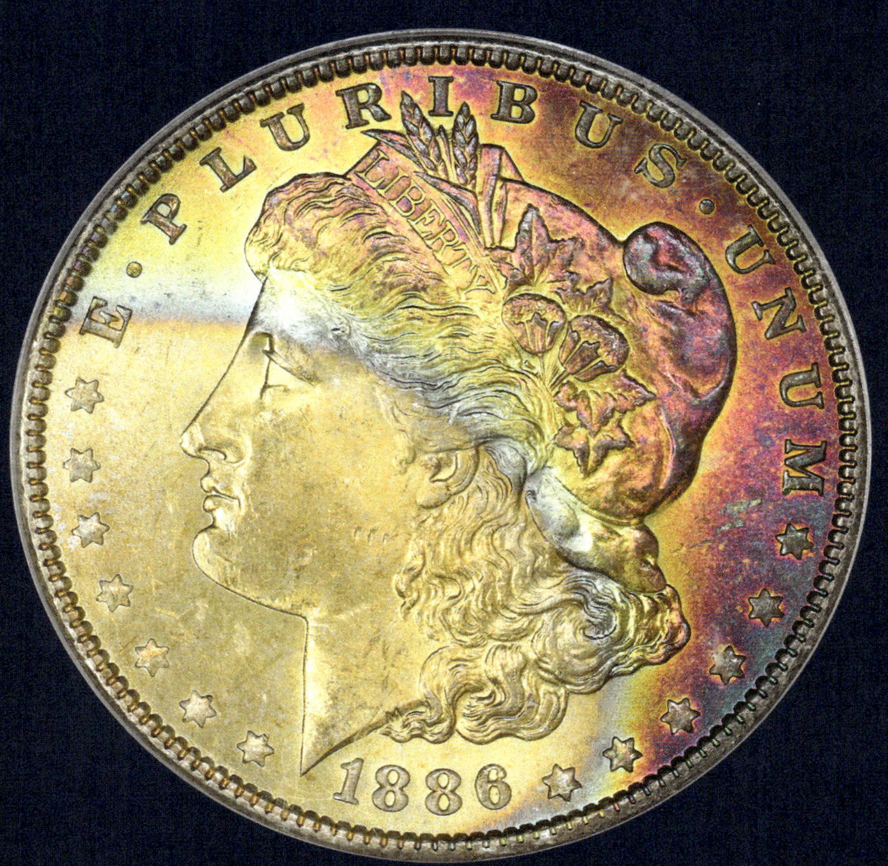

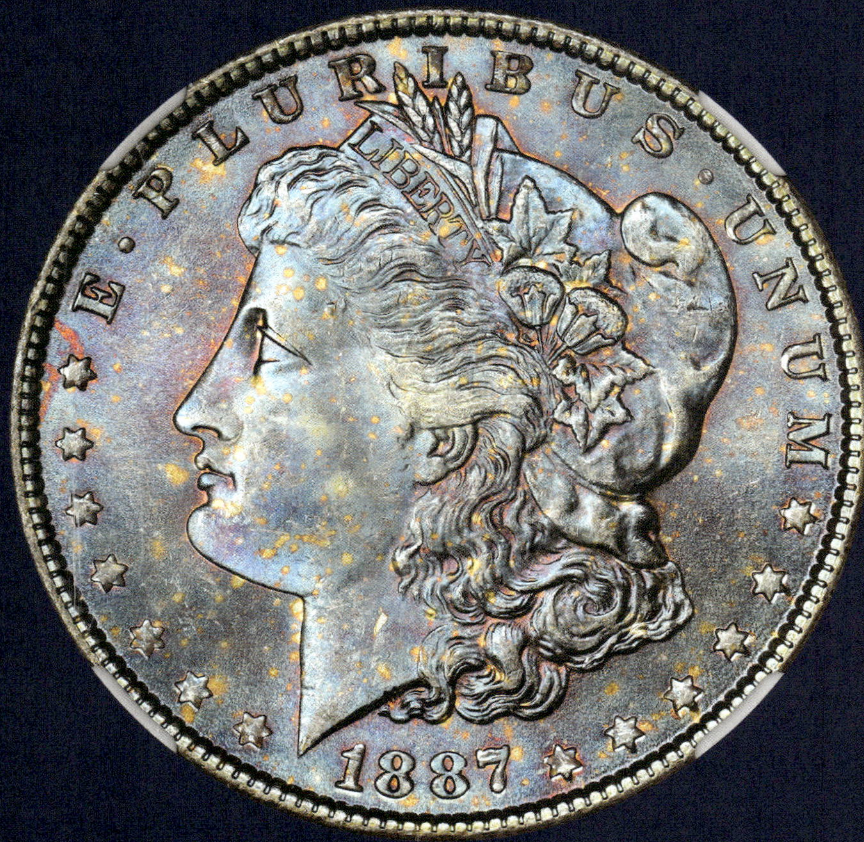

1886 $1 PCGS MS64
Certification number 3475372

"The Blueberry"
1887 $1 NGC MS65
Certification number 4652103-004

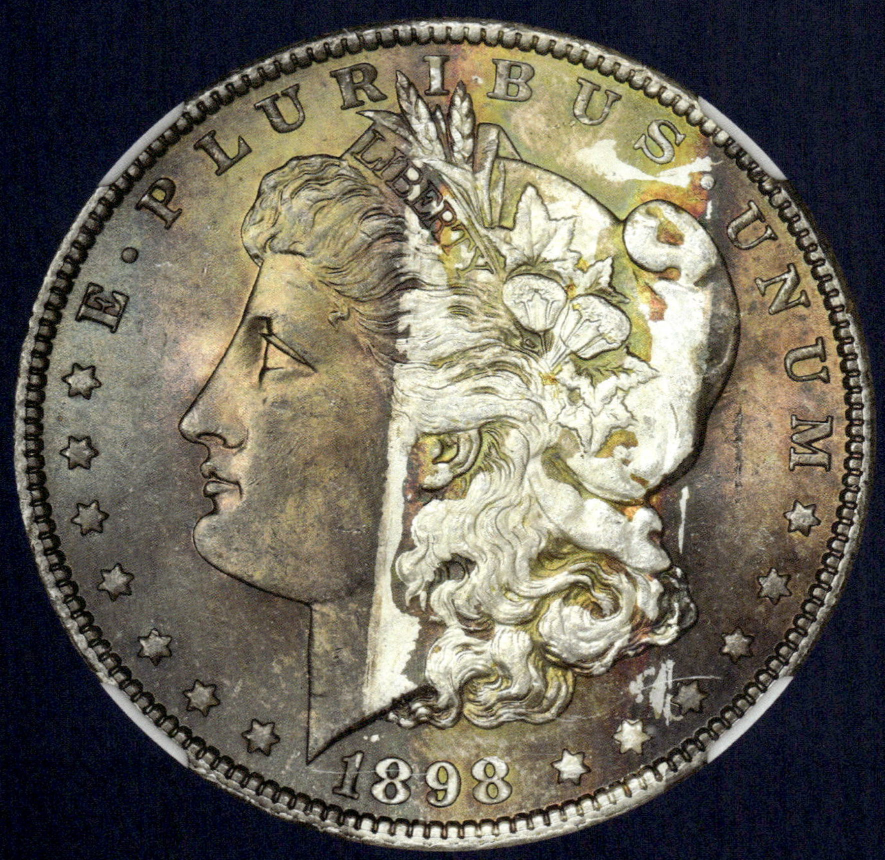

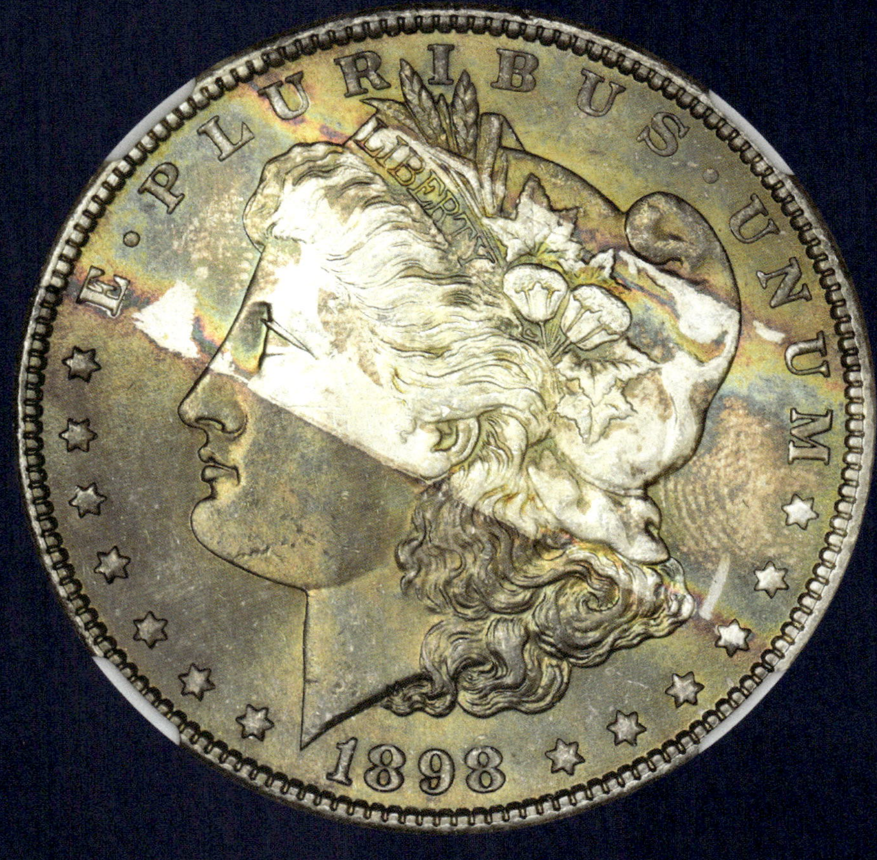

1898 $1 NGC MS63
Certification number 4963427-004

1898 $1 NGC MS63
Certification number 4963427-007

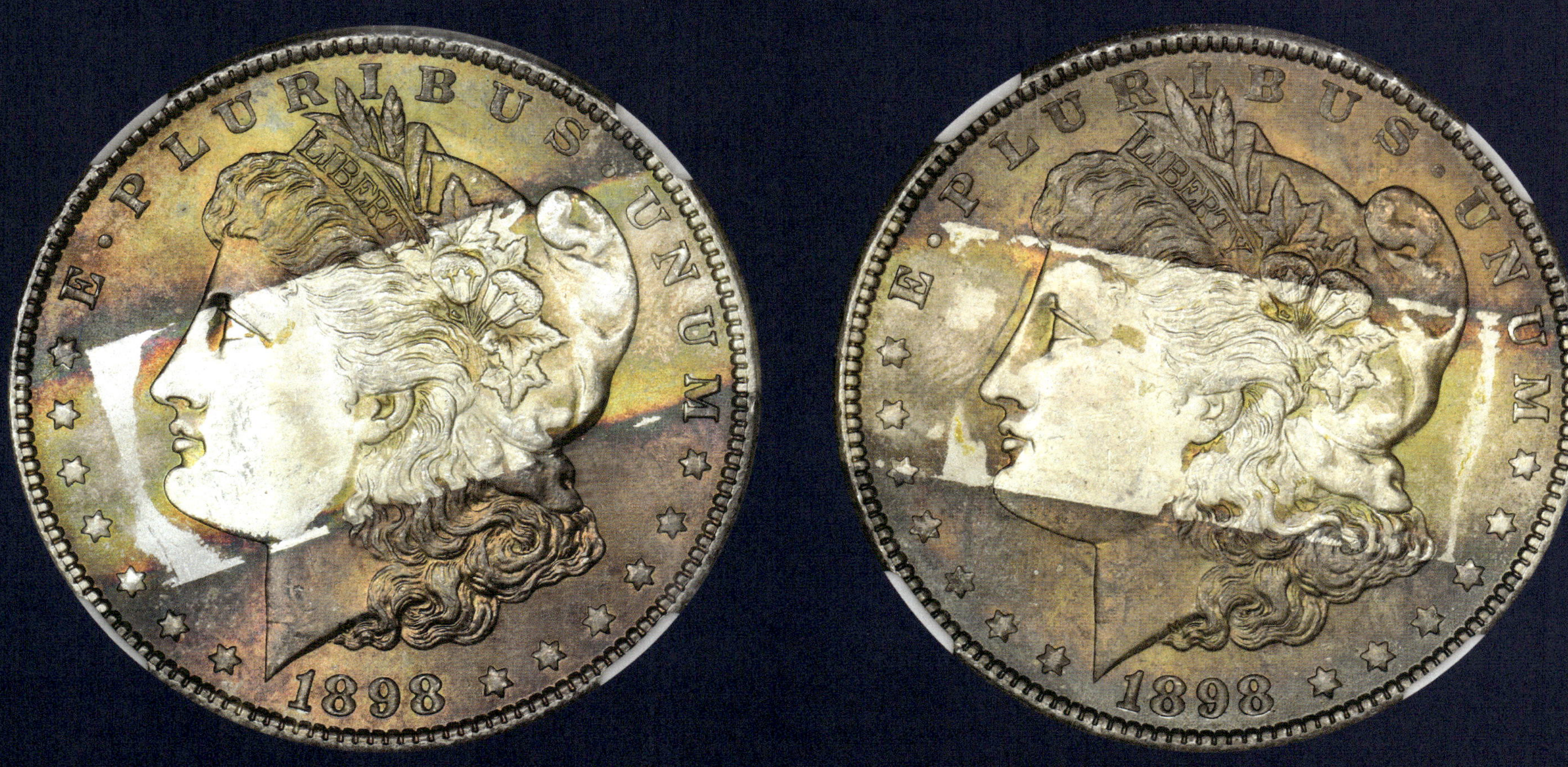

1898 $1 NGC MS63
Certification number 4963427-005

1898 $1 NGC MS63
Certification number 4963427-006

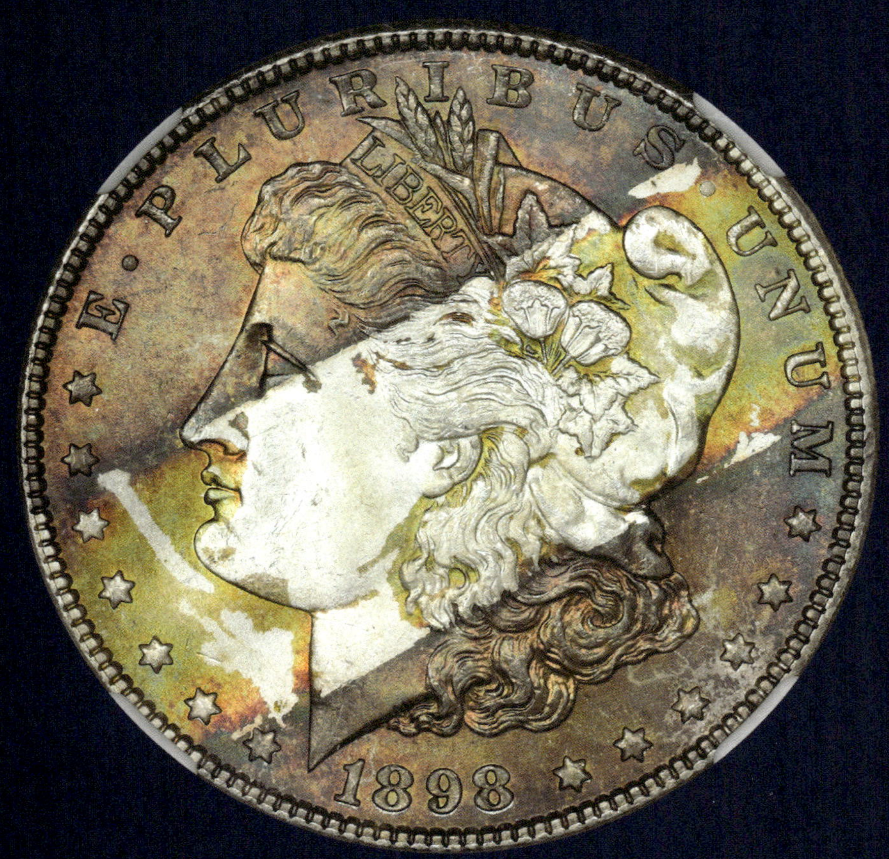

1898 $1 NGC MS63
Certification number 4963427-008

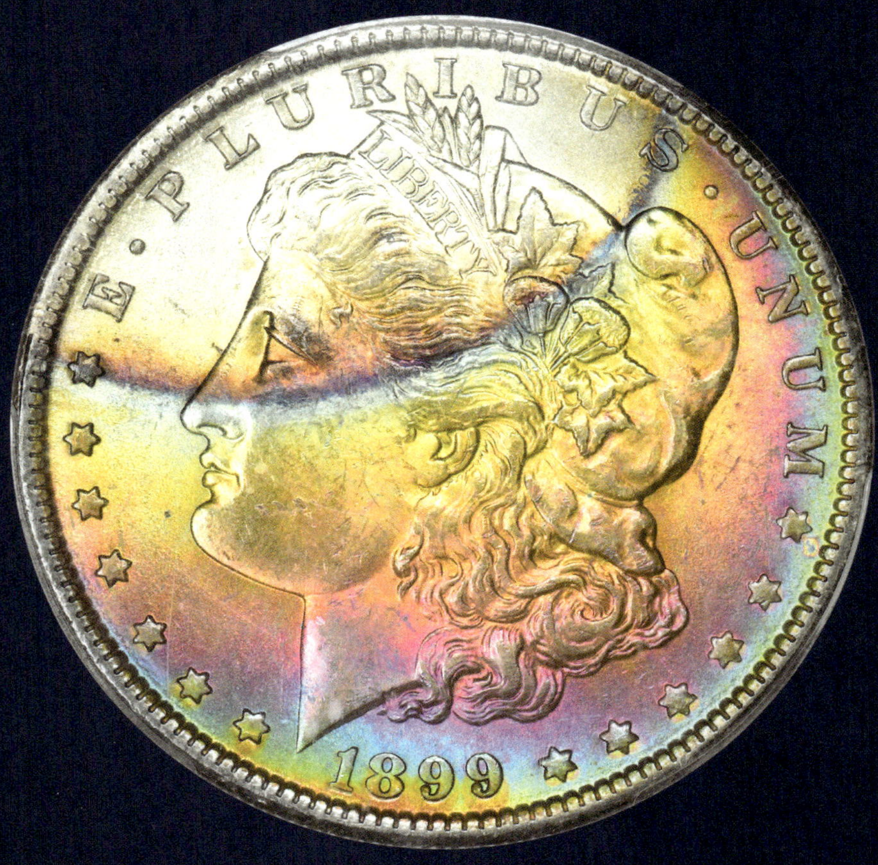

1899-O $1 PCGS MS64
Certification number 80550012

Chapter 2

Morgan Dollars - Reverse Toned

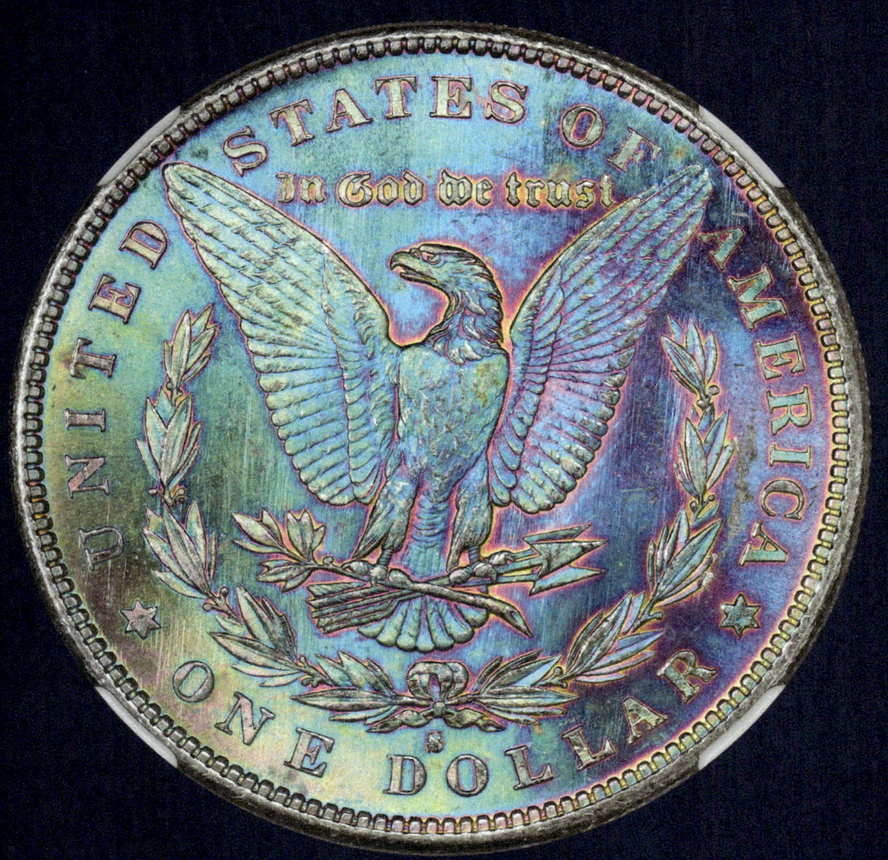

1879-S $1 NGC MS63★
Certification number 1803170-002

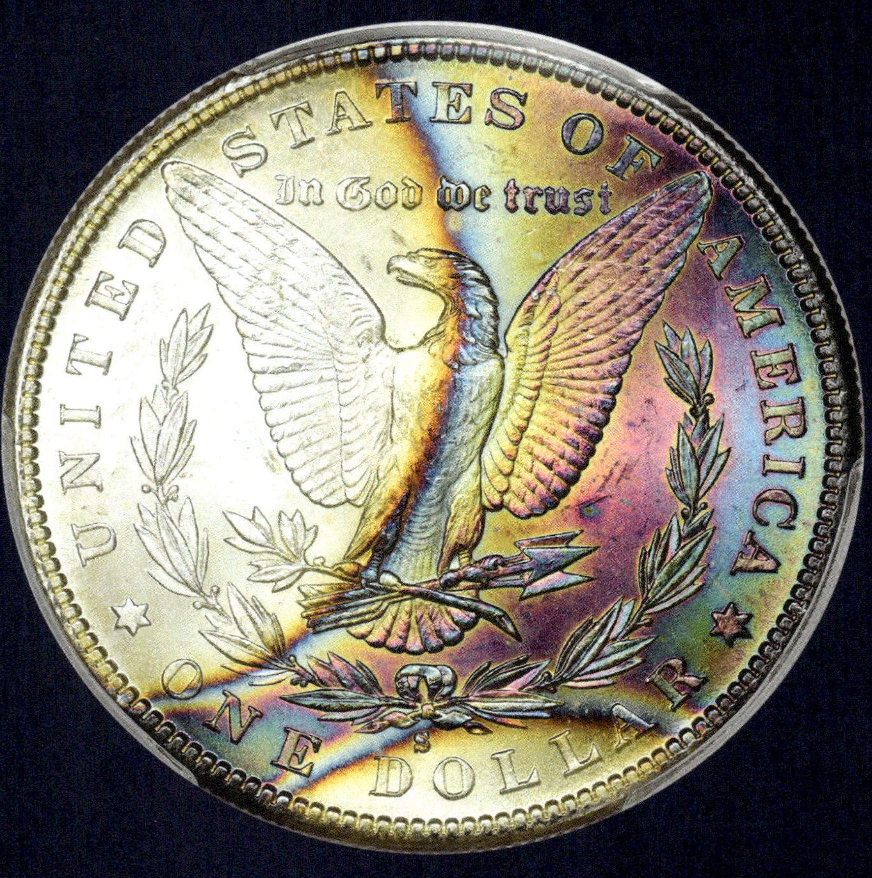

“Whale Tail #1”
1881-S $1 PCGS MS65
Certification number 30732427

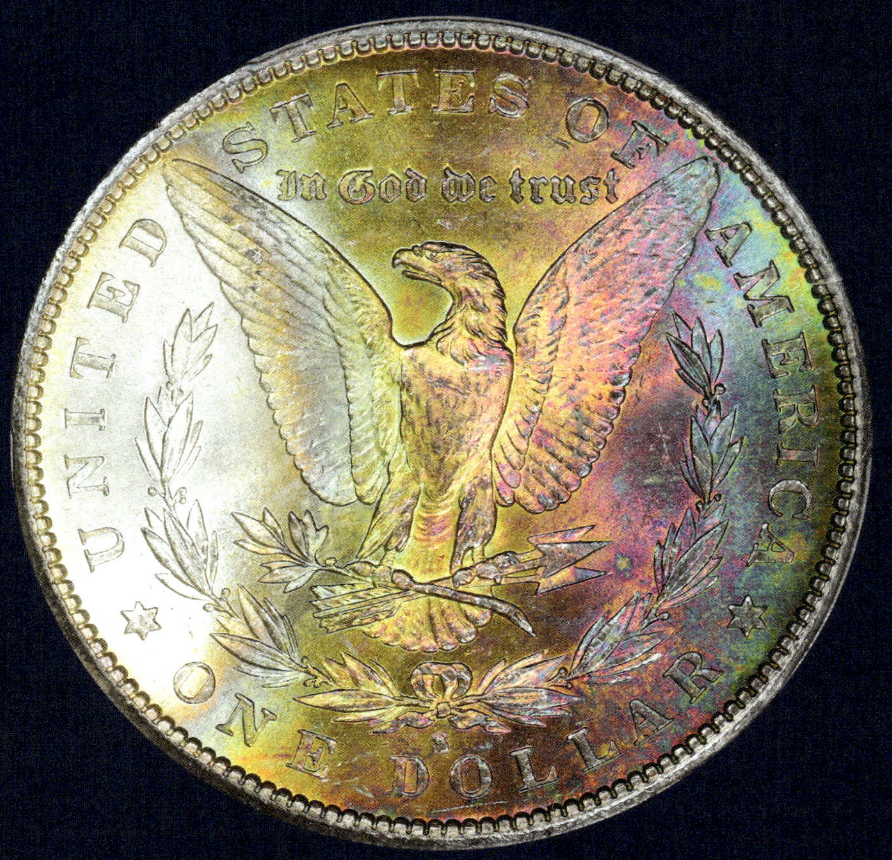

1881-S $1 PCGS MS66
Certification number 36651371

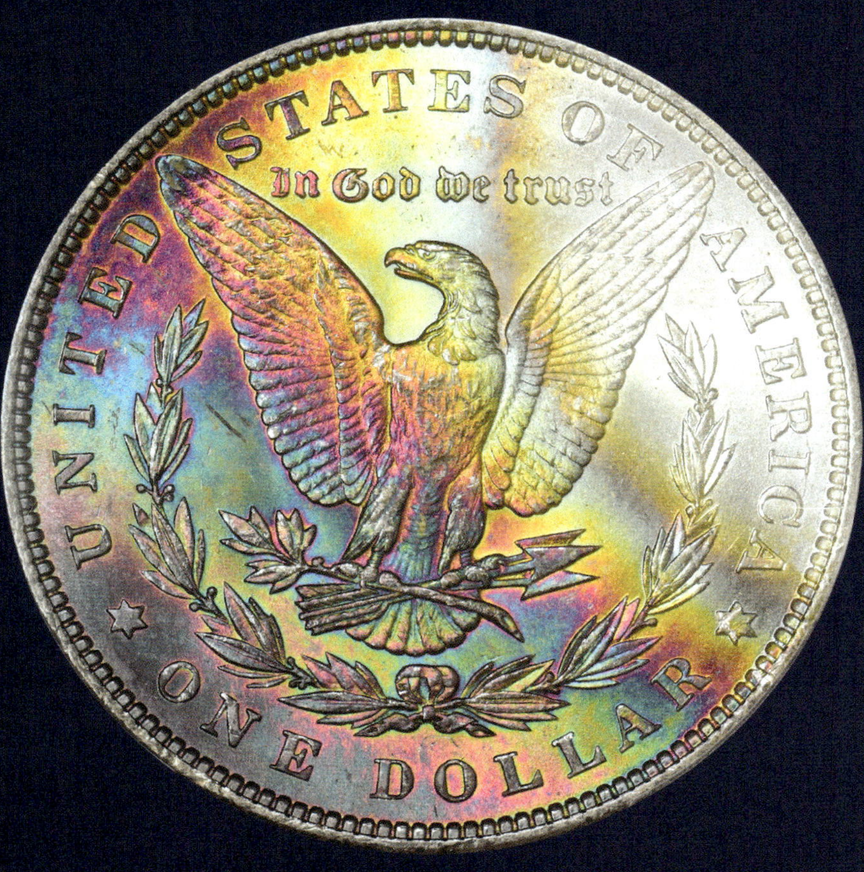

1883 $1 PCGS MS66
Certification number 81475456

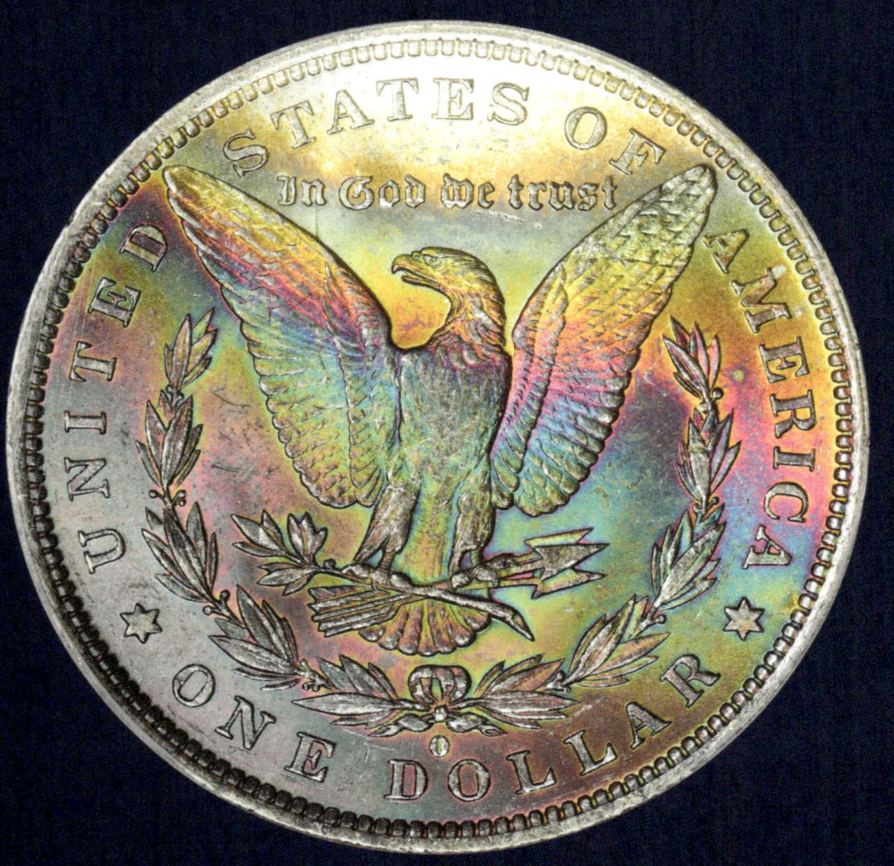

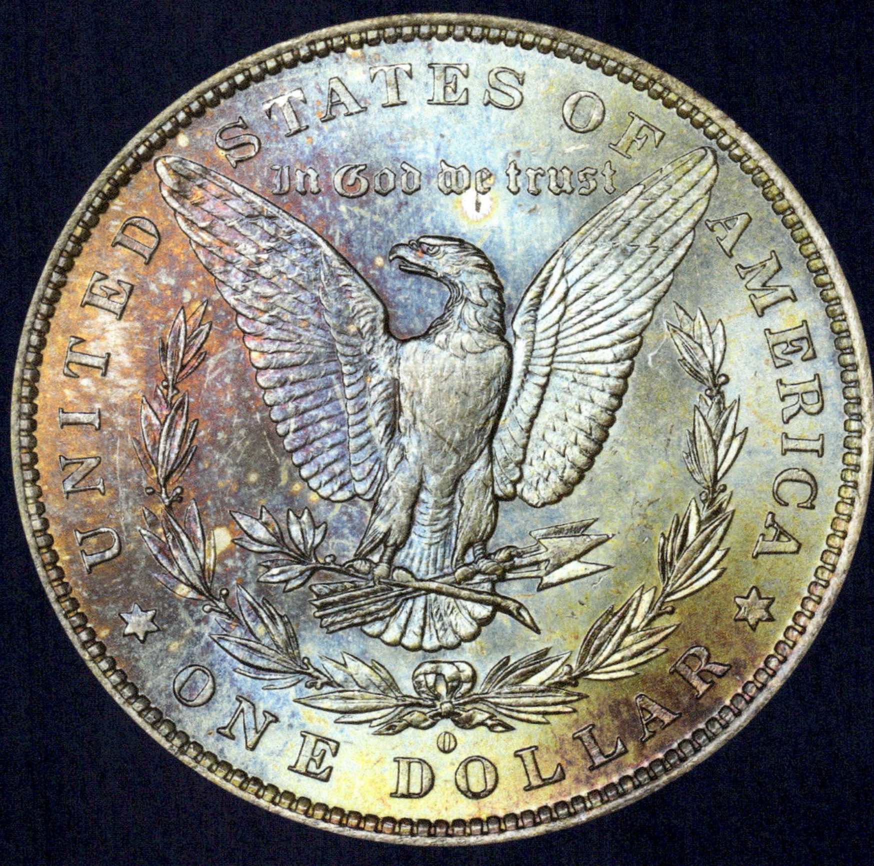

1883-O $1 PCGS MS63
Certification number 82207623

1883-O $1 NGC MS63★
Certification number 1985379-005
Ex. Great Montana Collection

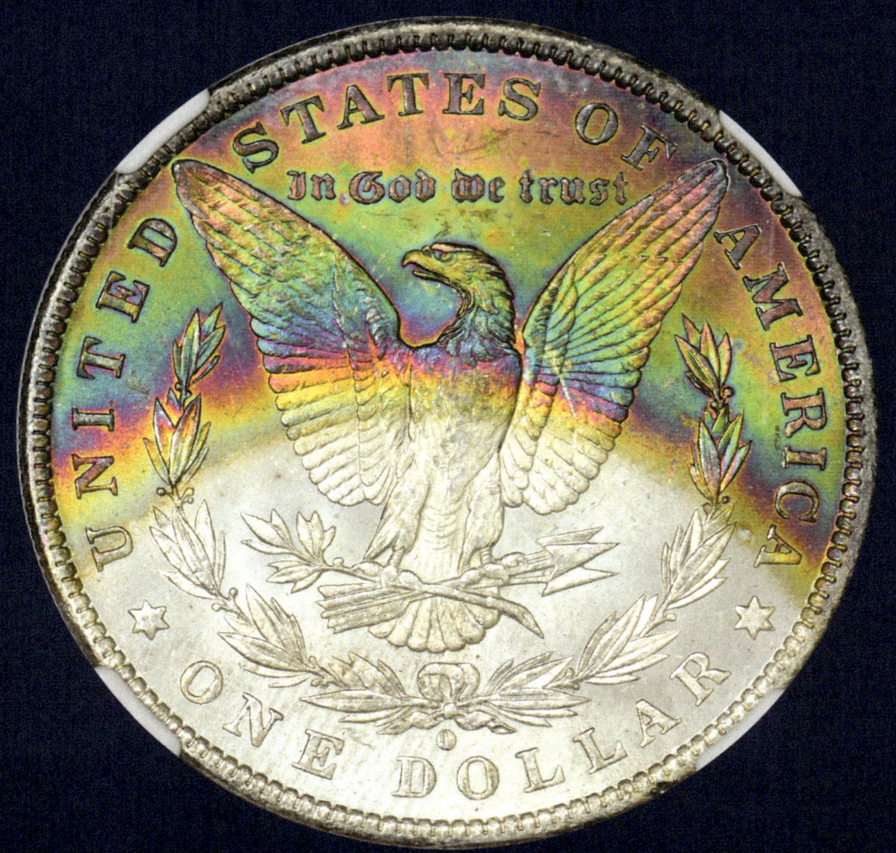

1883-O $1 NGC MS64★
Certification number 2382137-004

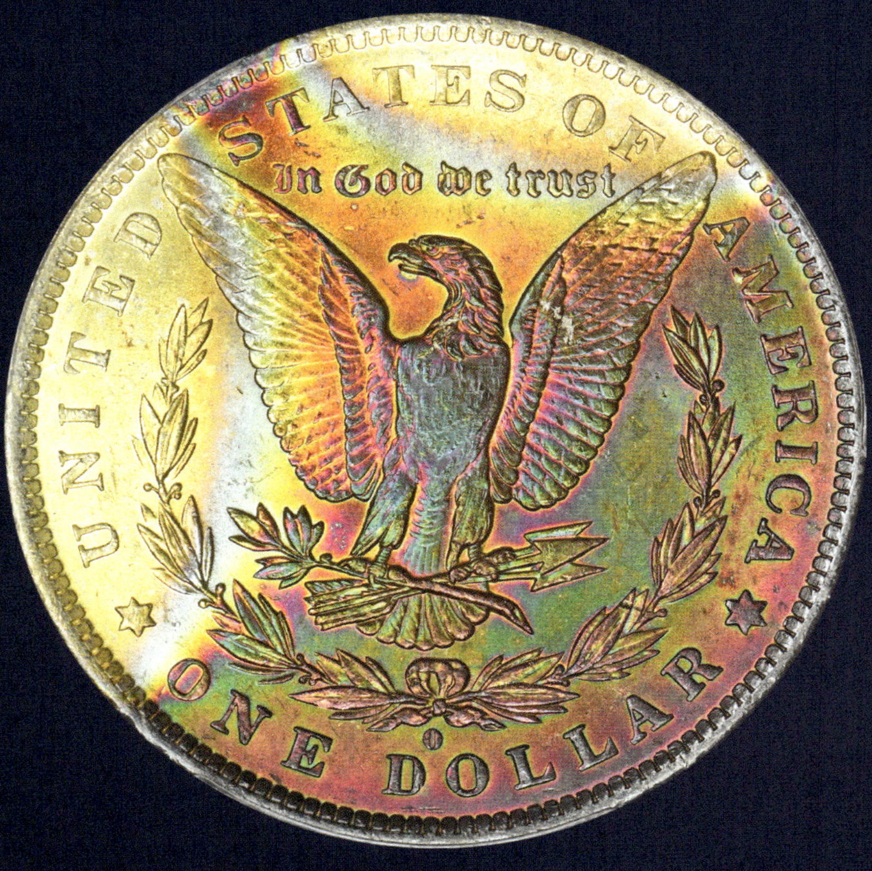

"Whale Tail #2"
1883-O $1 PCGS MS64
Certification number 82419209

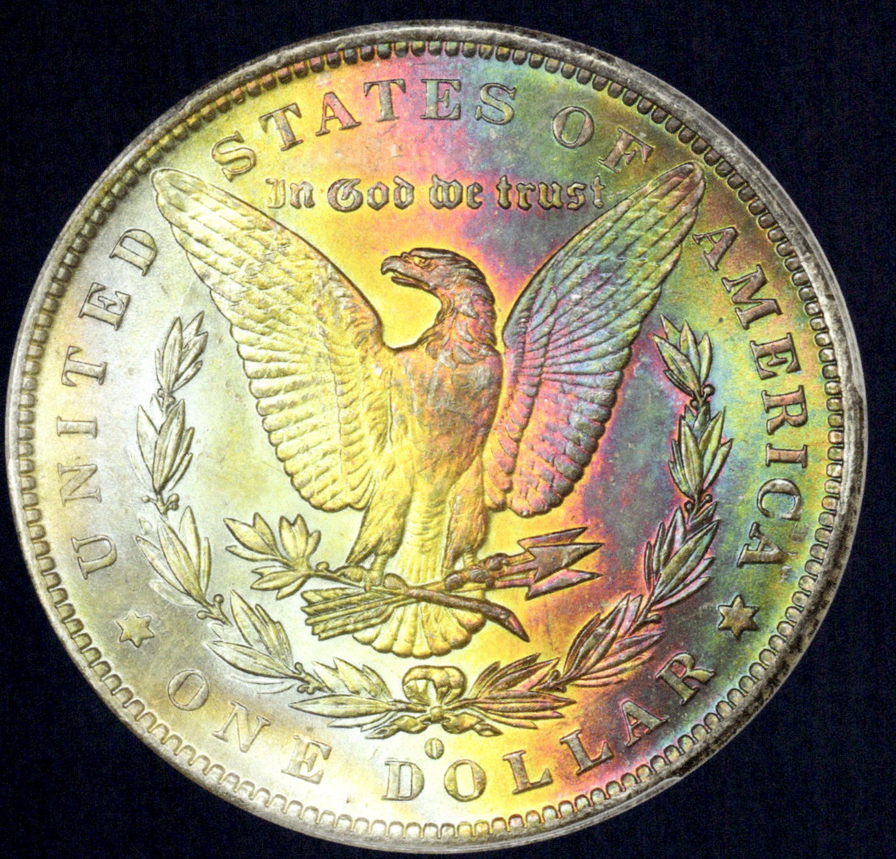

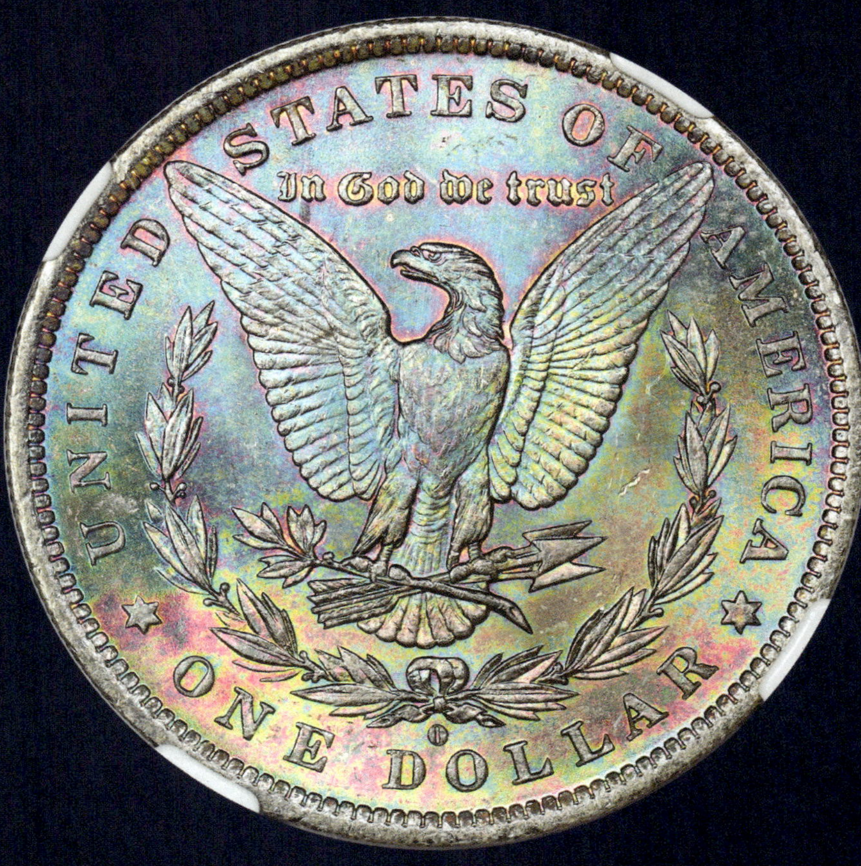

1883-O $1 PCGS MS66
Certification number 29750814

1884-O $1 NGC MS63★
Certification number 350015-049

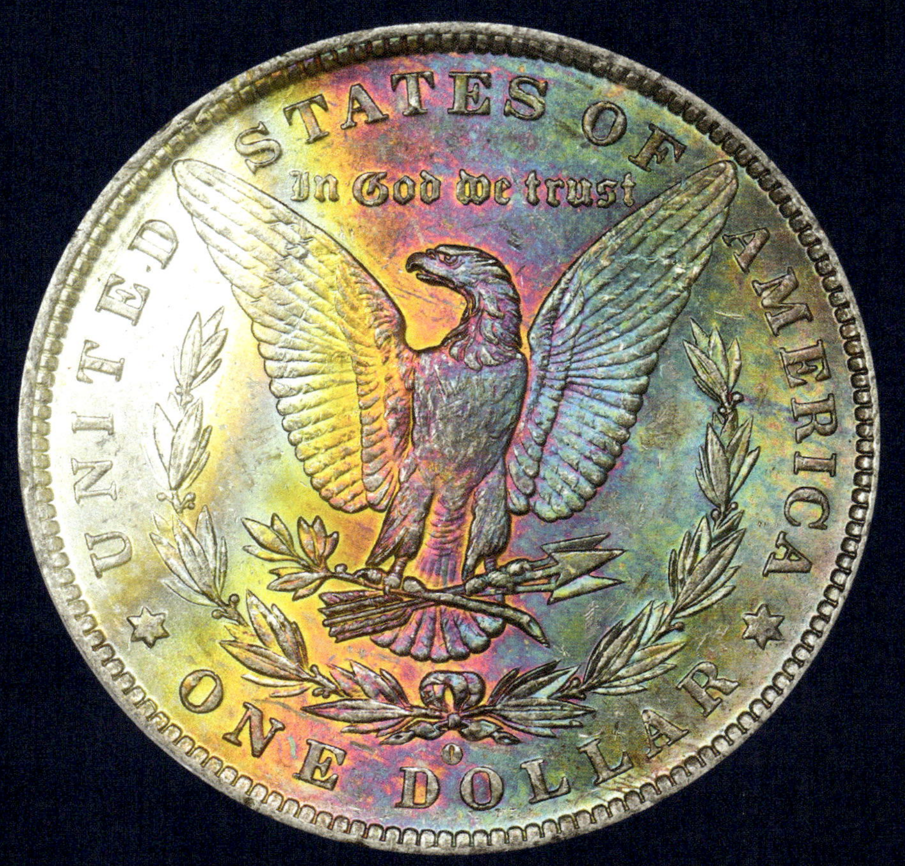

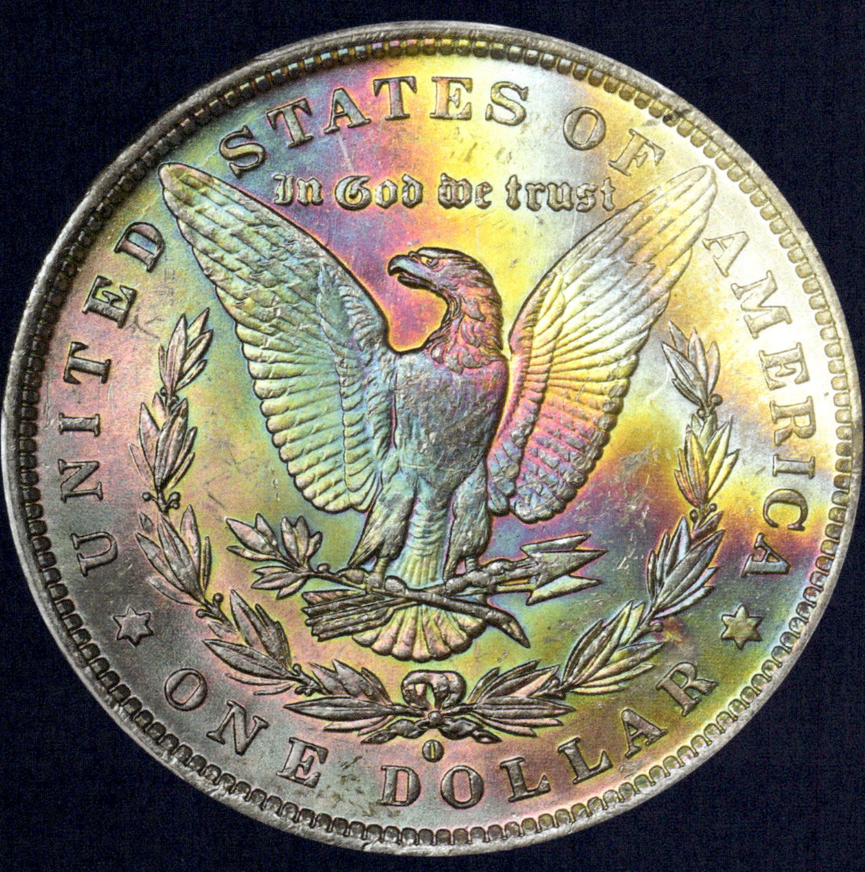

1884-O $1 PCGS MS63
Certification number 29409548

1884-O $1 PCGS MS65
Certification number 83942777

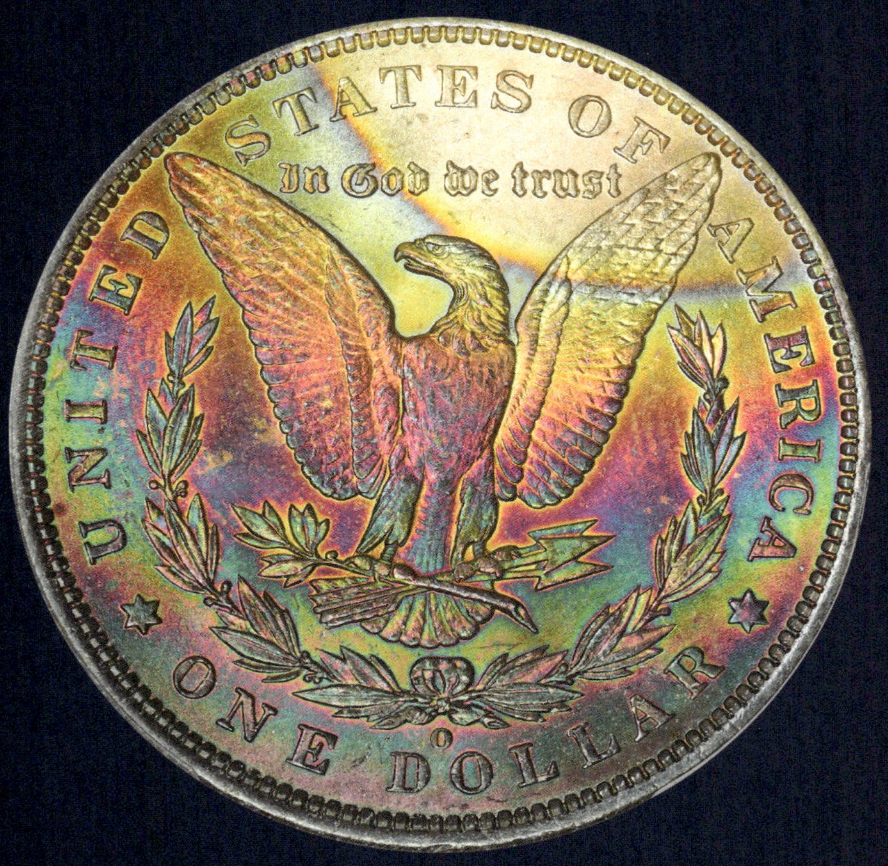

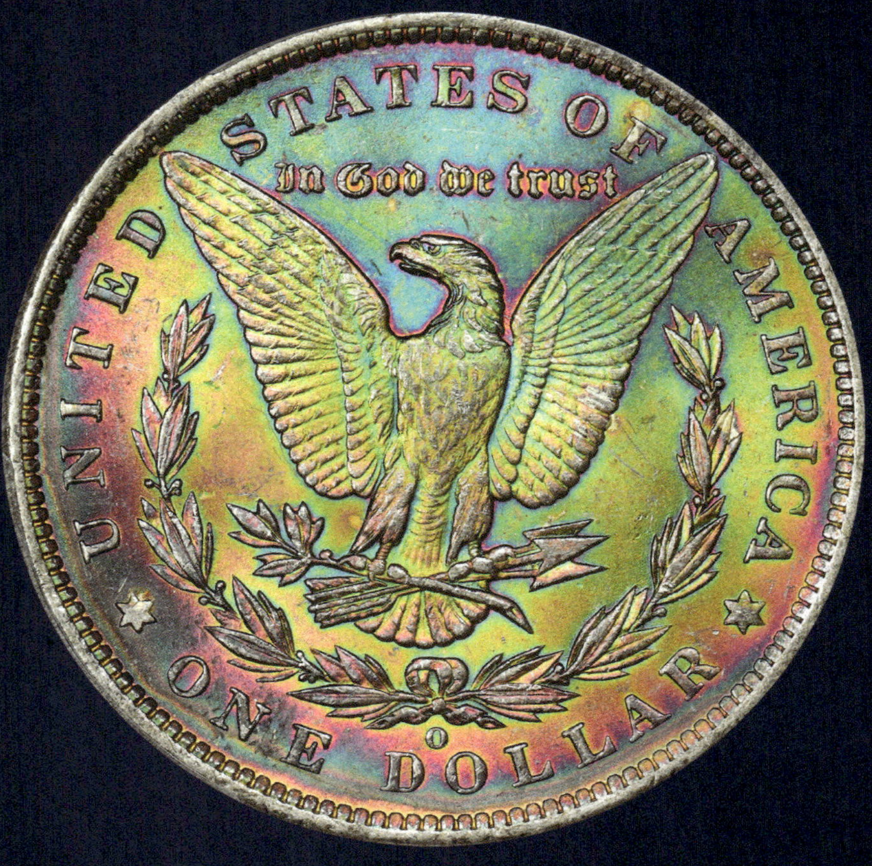

1884-O $1 PCGS MS65
Certification number 34657136

1885-O $1 PCGS MS63
Certification number 36161366

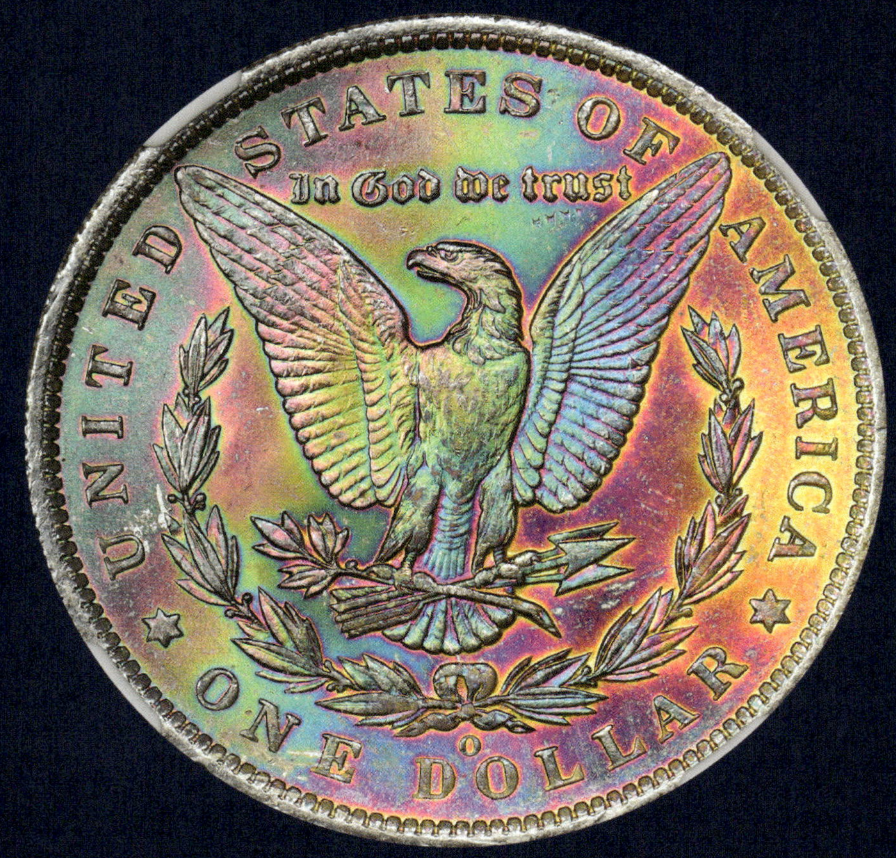

1885-O $1 NGC MS64★
Certification number 4297813-006

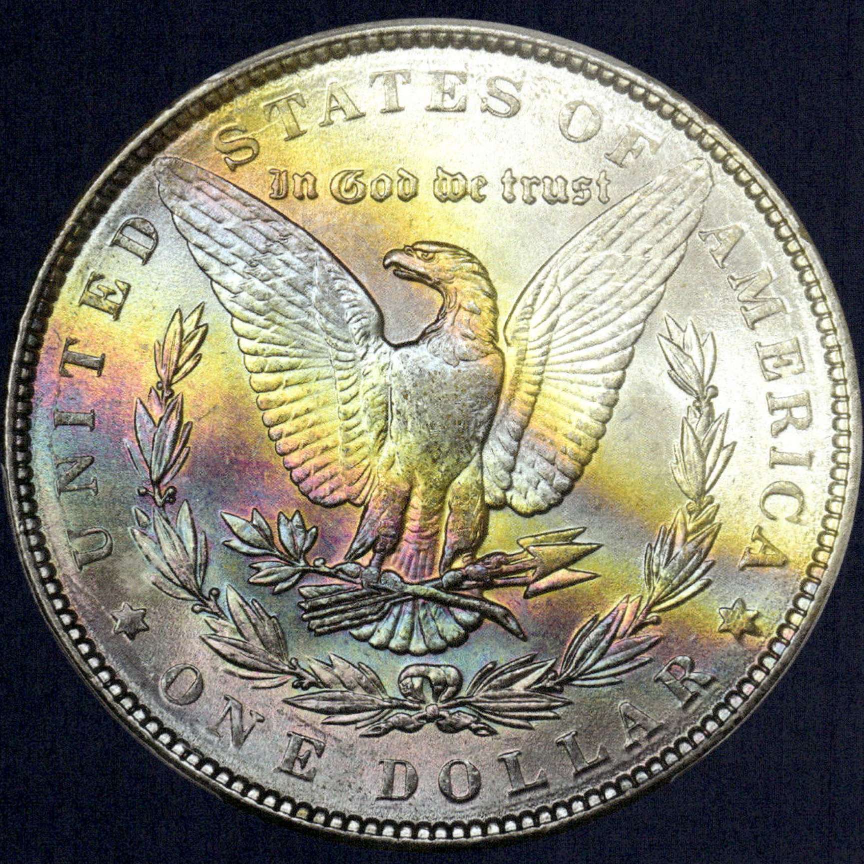

1886 $1 PCGS MS66
Certification number 84025929

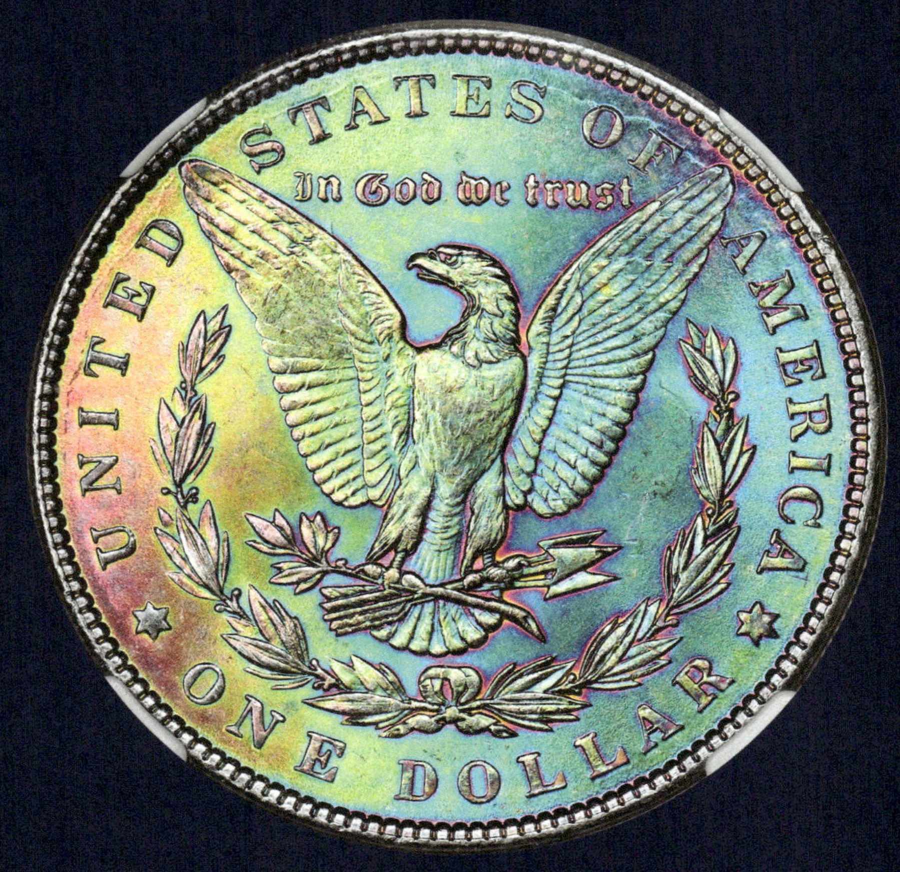

1887 $1 NGC MS64★
Certification number 1864750-02
Ex. Battle Creek Collection

Chapter 3

Eisenhower Dollars

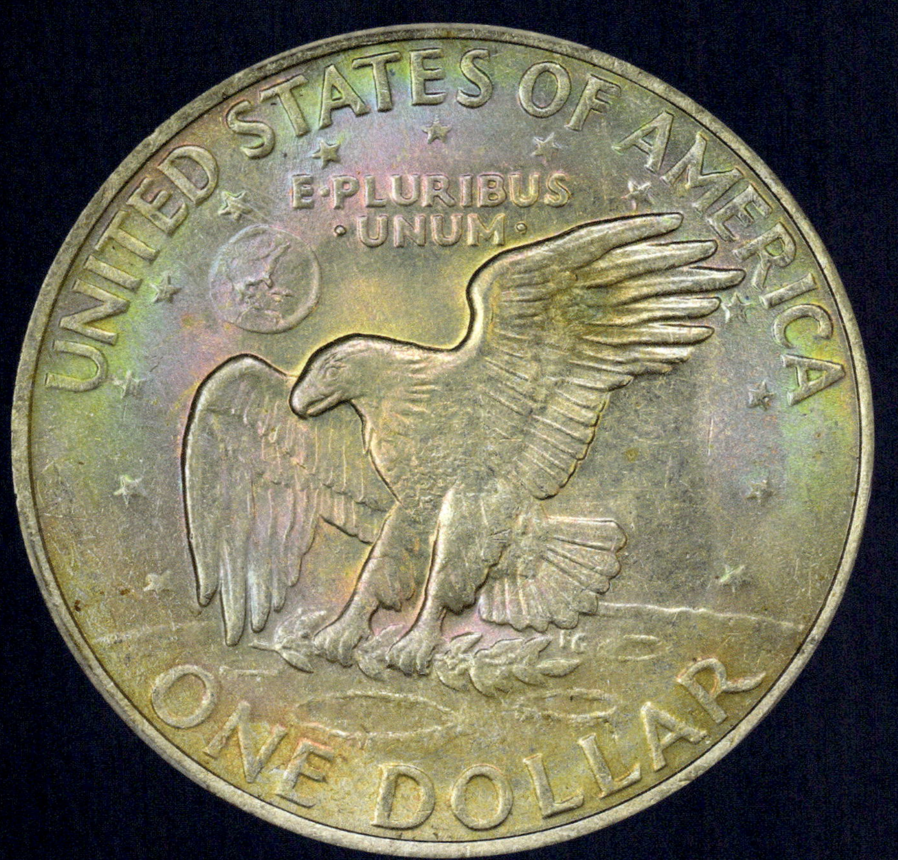

1971 $1 PCGS MS64
Certification number 38289420

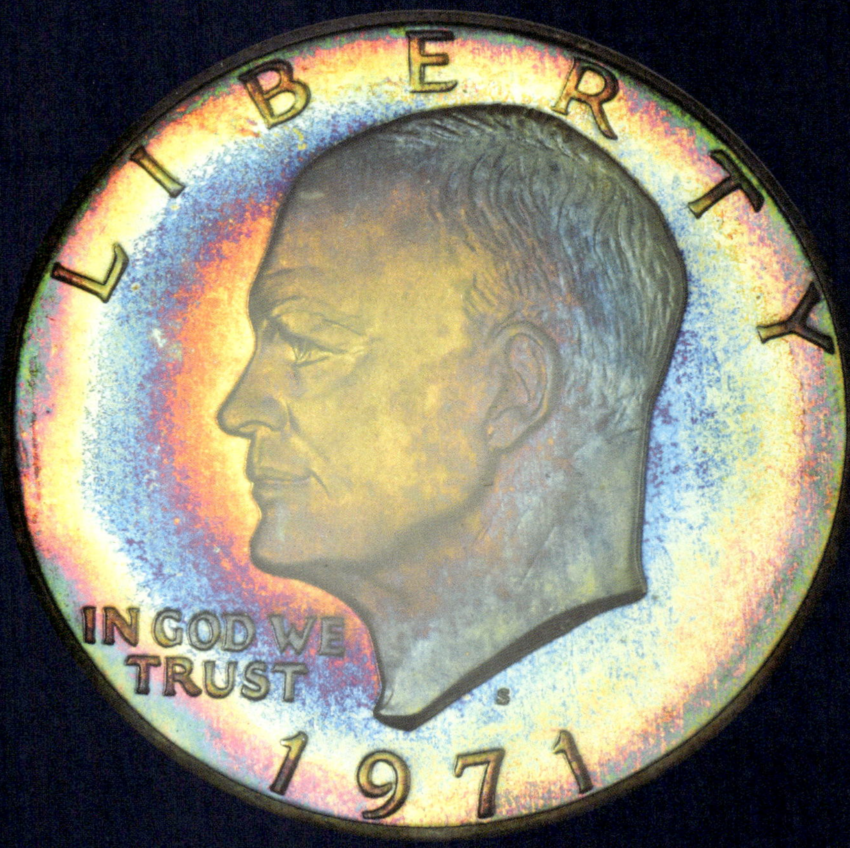

1971-S $1 PCGS PR67DCAM
Certification number 29867167

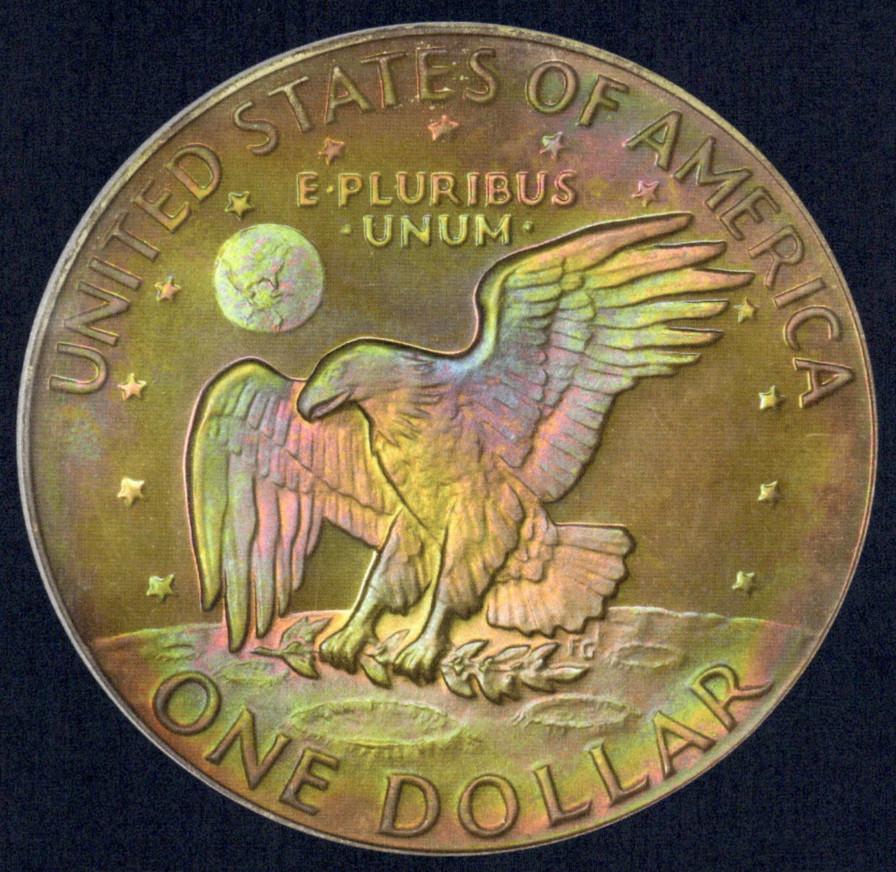

"Rainbow Eagle"
1978-S $1 PCGS PR66CAM
Certification number 33373493

Chapter 4

American Silver Eagles

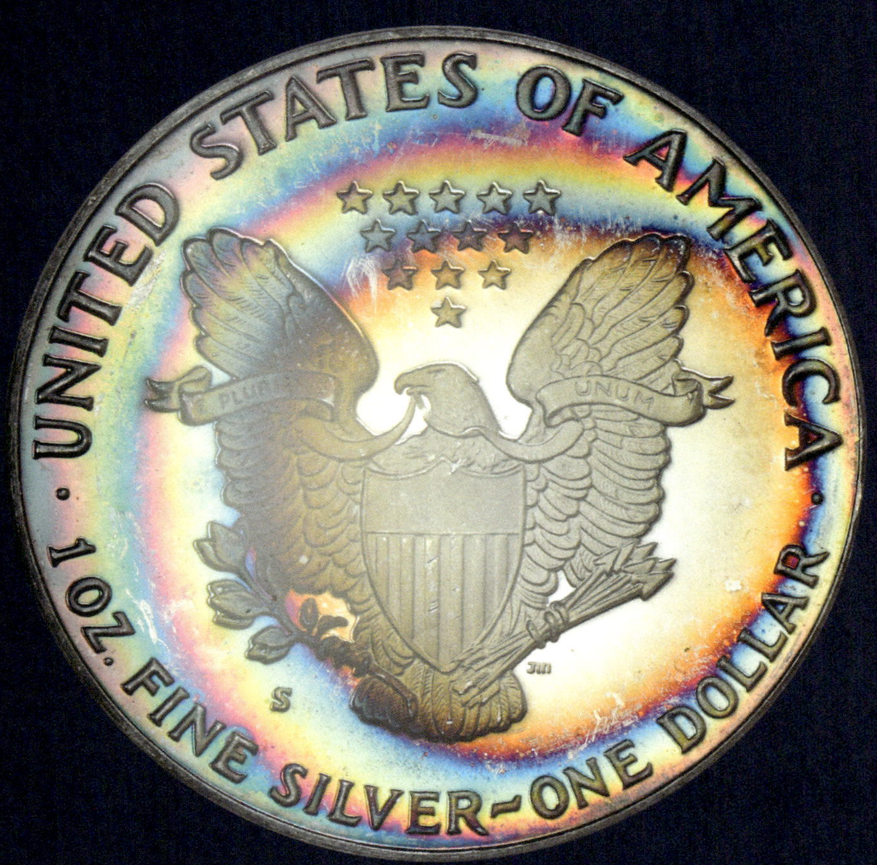

1987-S $1 PCGS PR67DCAM
Certification number 32439801

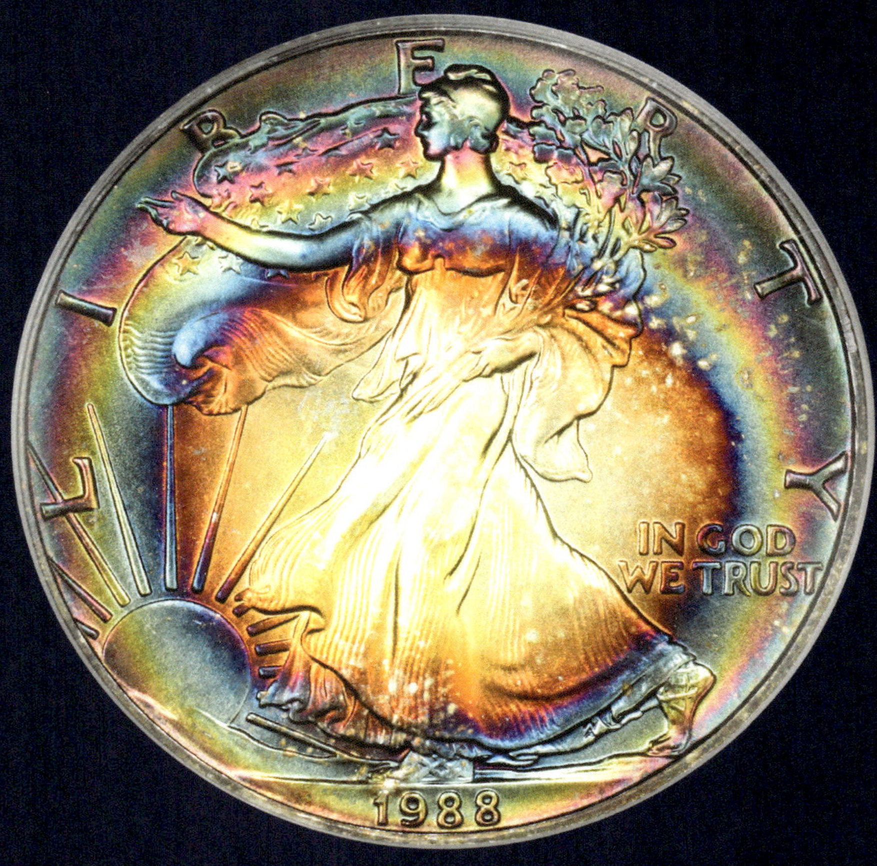

"Pink-Handed Lady"
1988 $1 PCGS MS68
Certification number 25662389

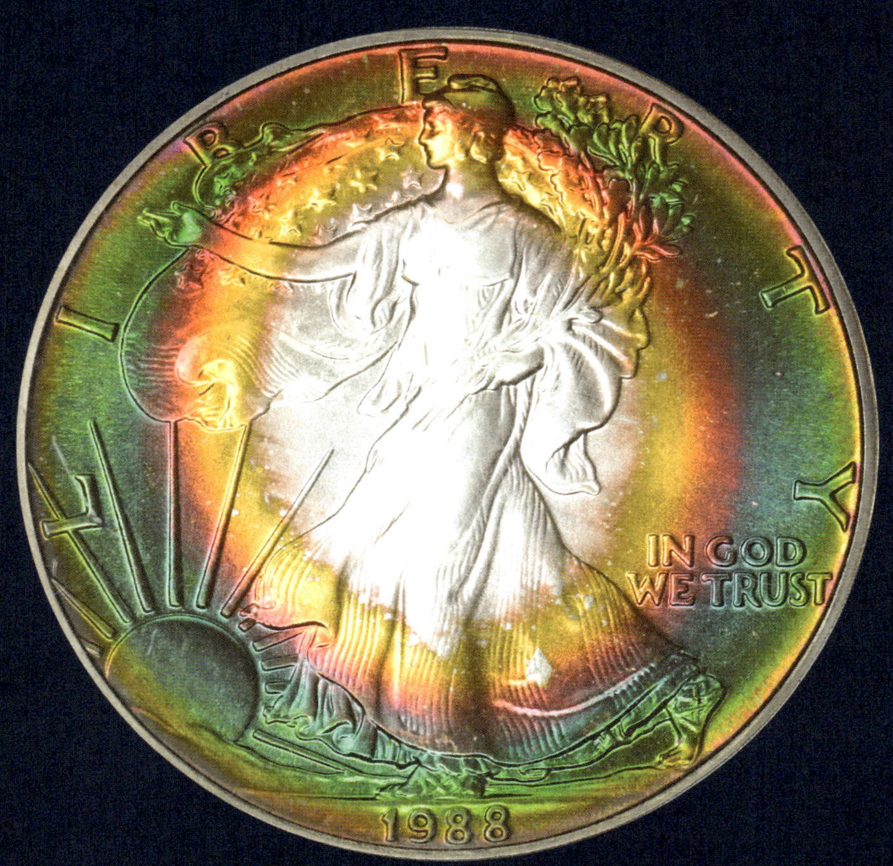

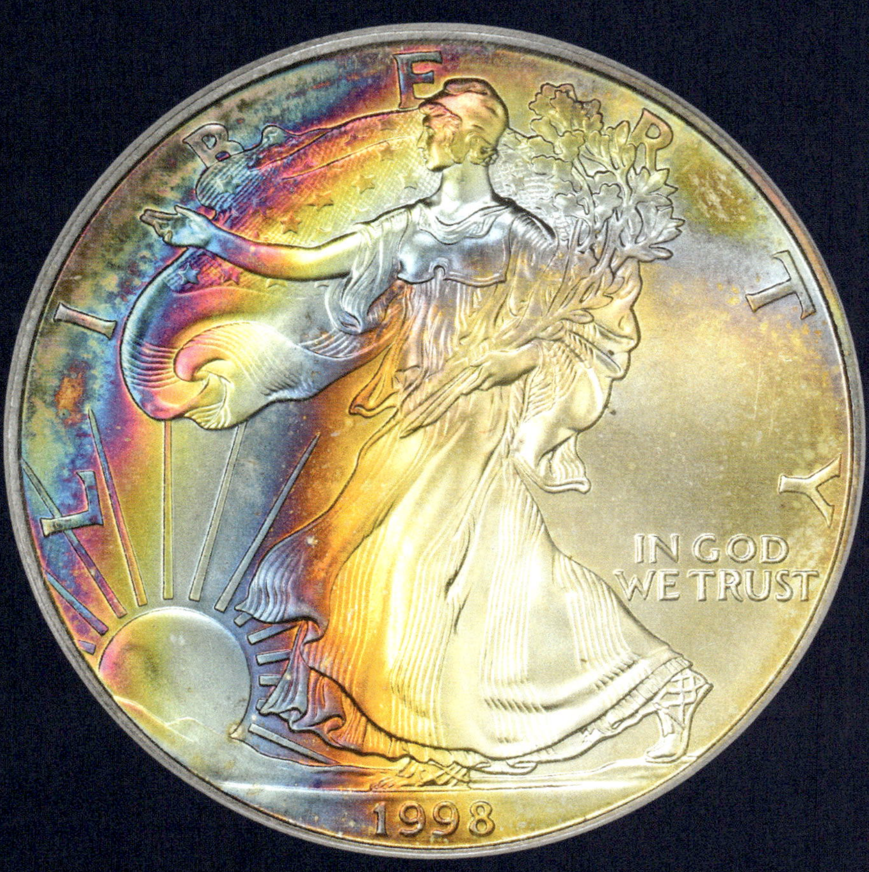

1988 $1 PCGS MS68
Certification number 37355575

"Dancing on Rainbows"
1998 $1 PCGS MS68
Certification number 35330421

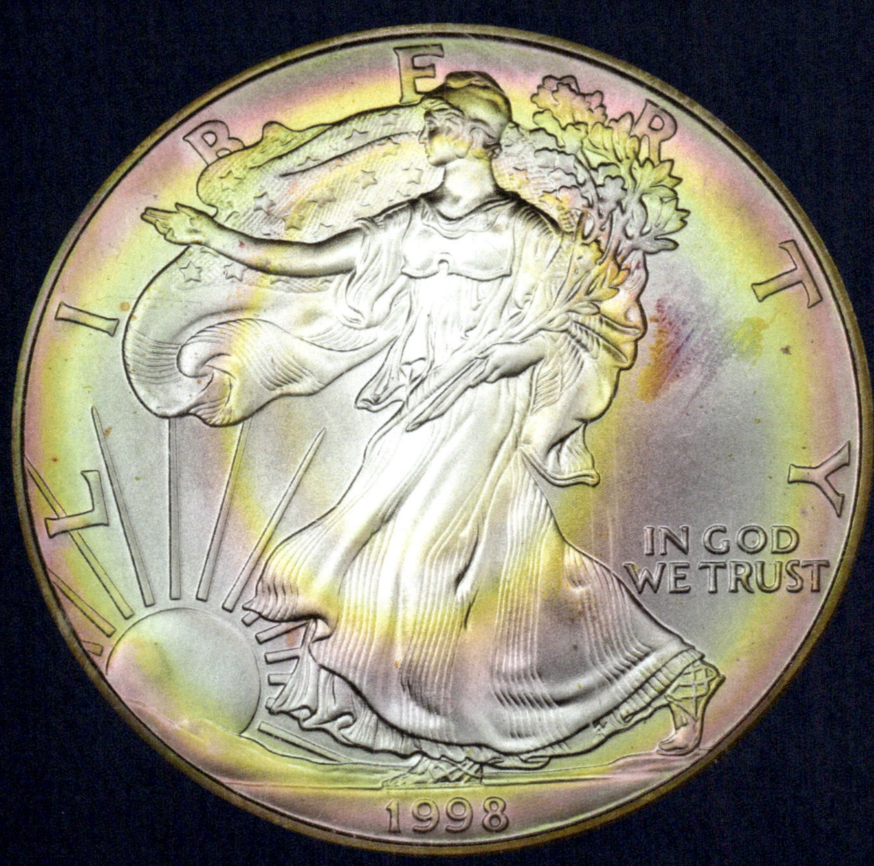

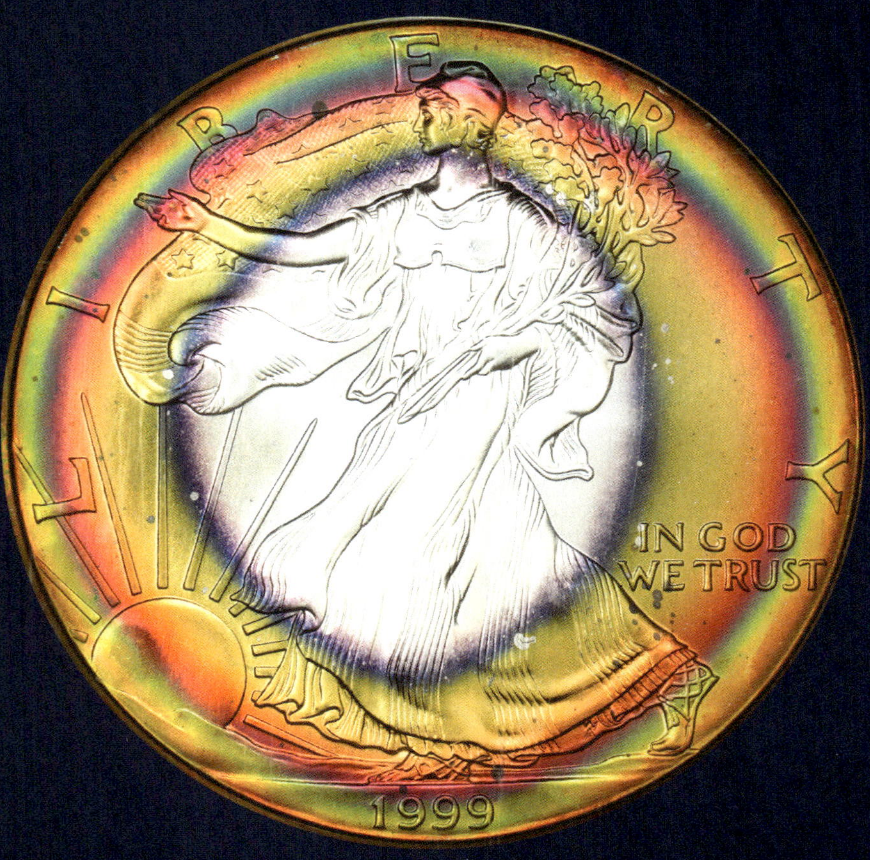

1998 $1 PCI MS67
Certification number 7978037210

1999 $1 PCI MS67
Certification number 8305496050

Chapter 5

Other U.S. Coins and Medals

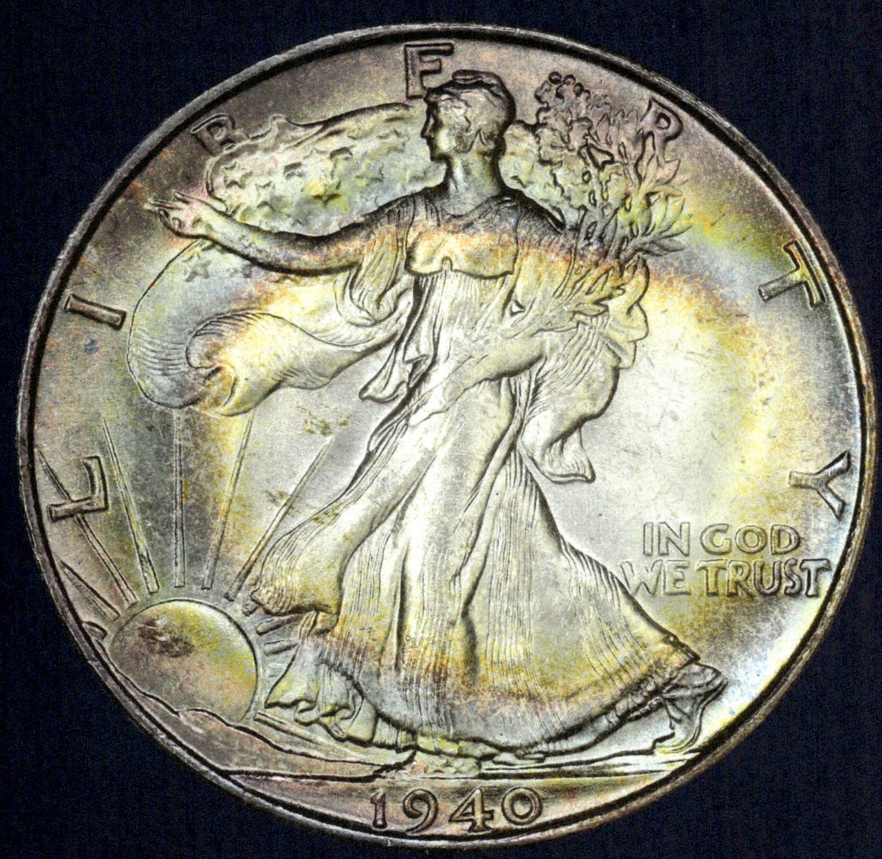

1940-S $.50 NGC MS65★
Certification number 4429606-001

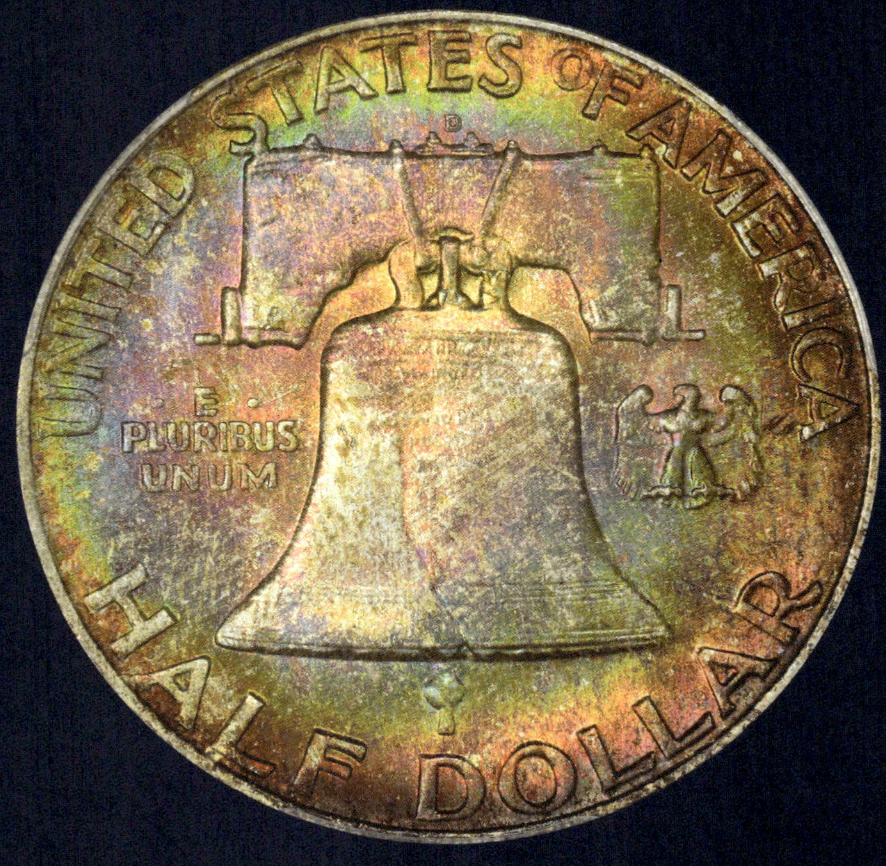

1953-D $.50 PCGS MS65FBL
Certification number 21268923

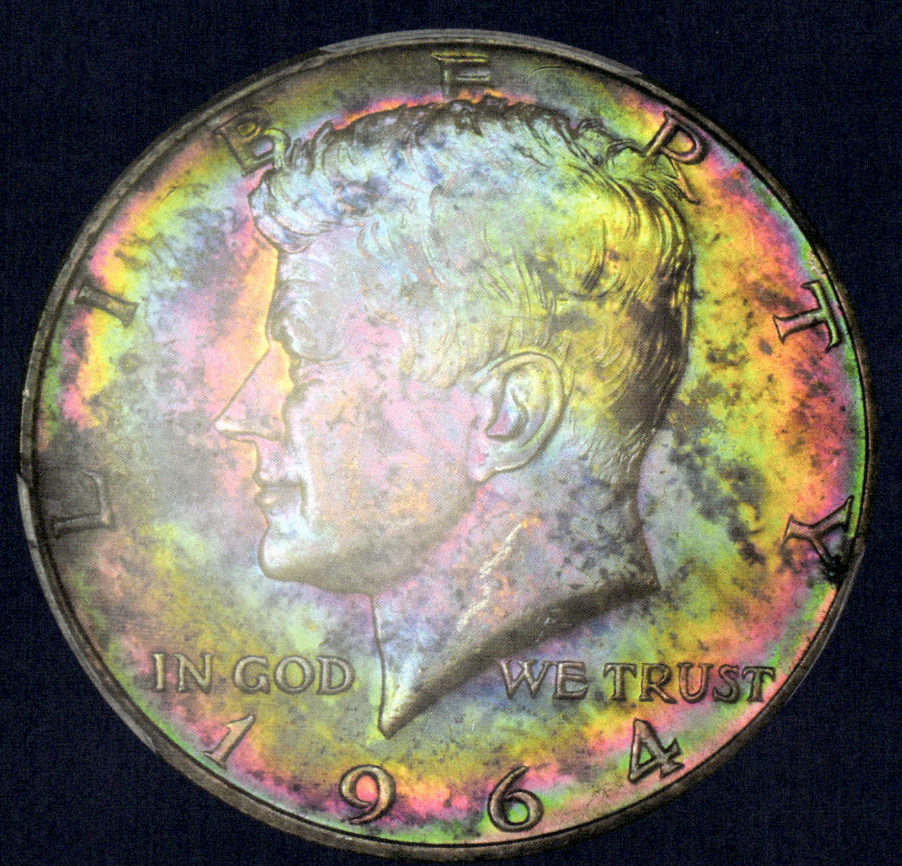

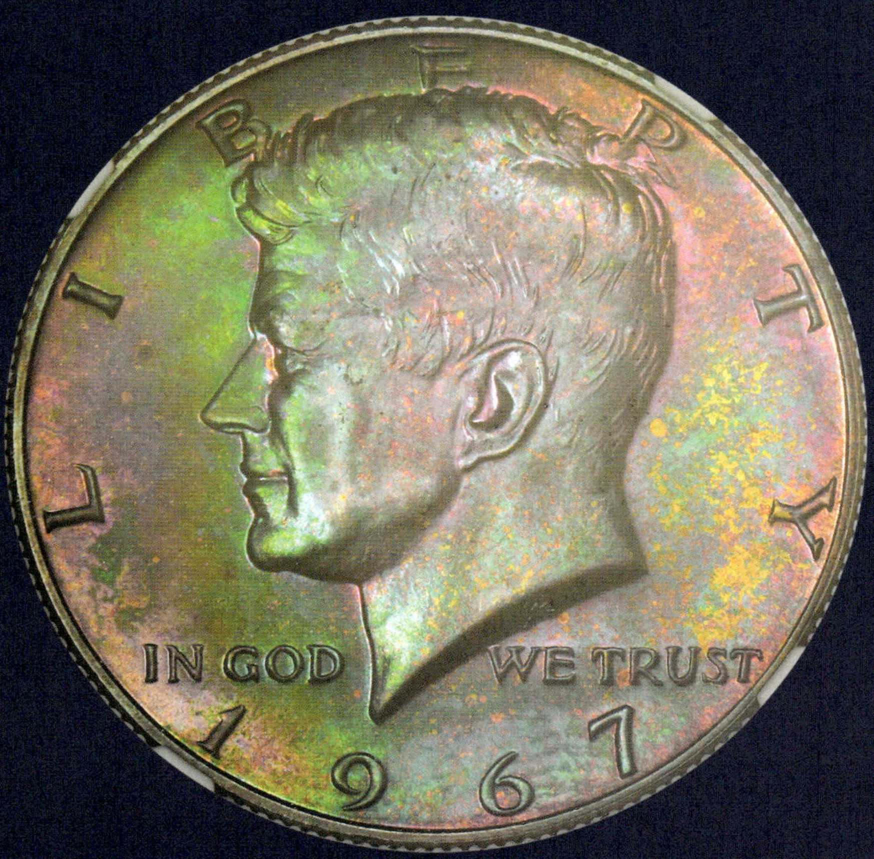

1964-D $.50 PCGS MS64
Certification number 80448282

1967 SMS $.50 NGC MS66
Certification number 4738888-013

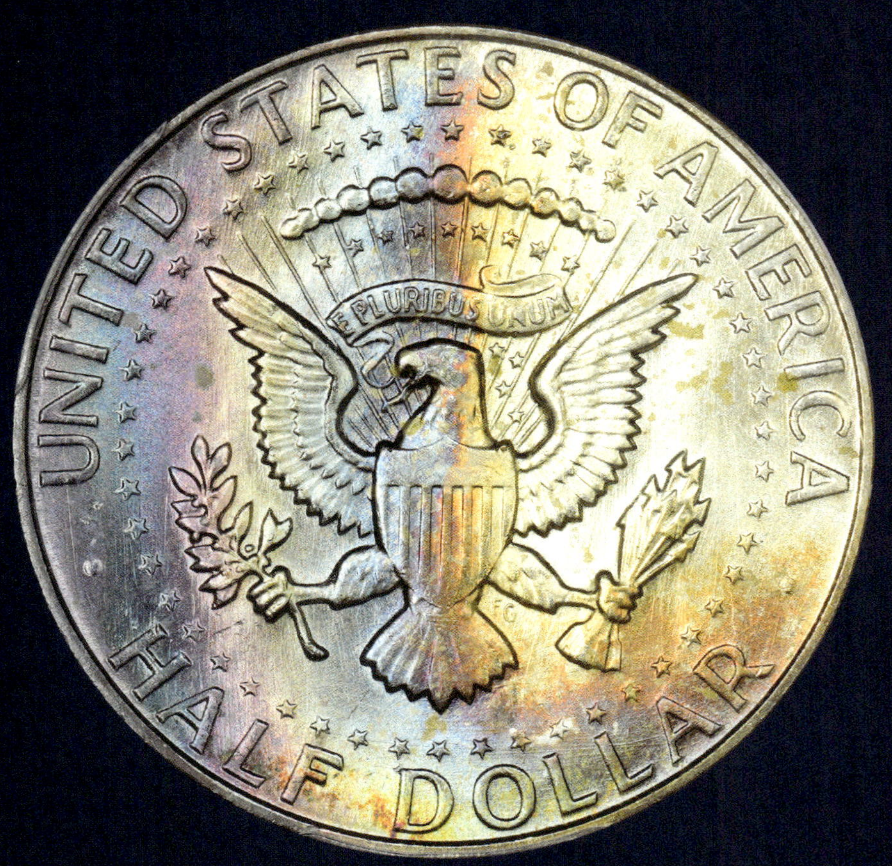

1968-D $.50 PCGS MS64
Certification number 34629627

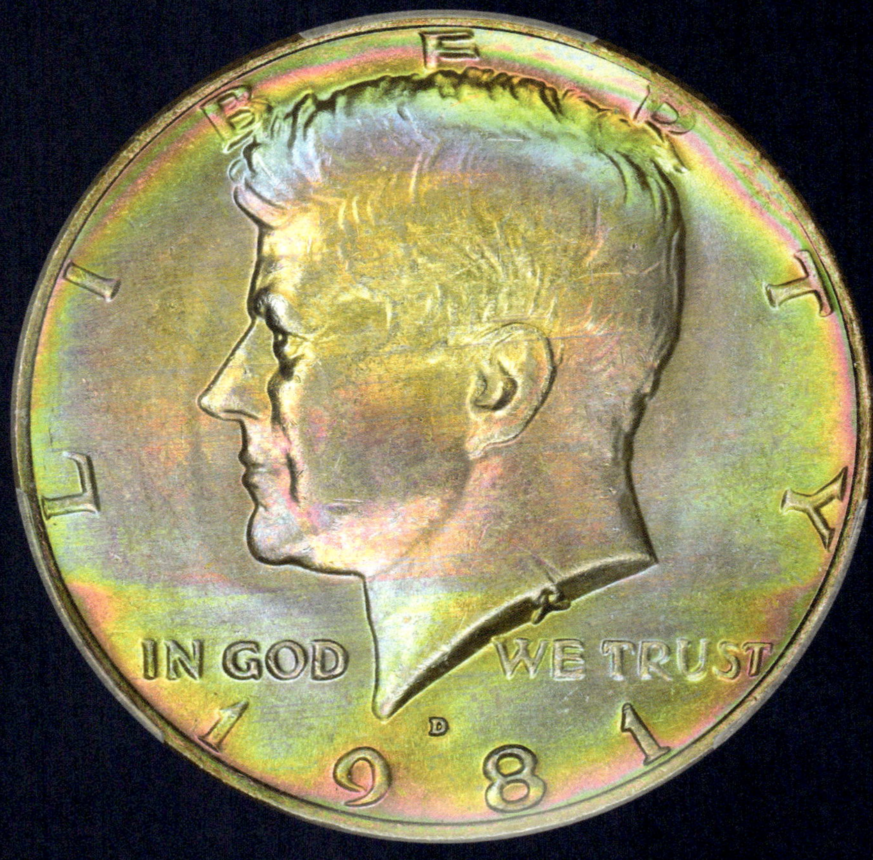

1981-D $.50 PCGS MS66
Certification number 38160860

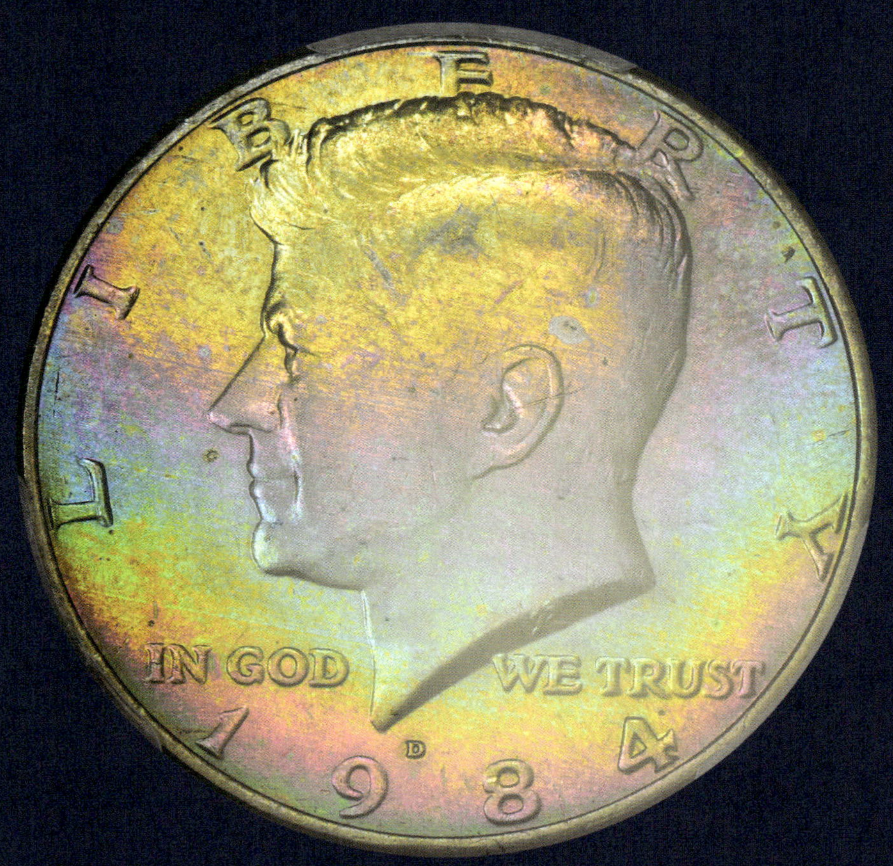

"Inside a Rainbow"
1984-D $.50 PCGS MS67
Certification number 82632045

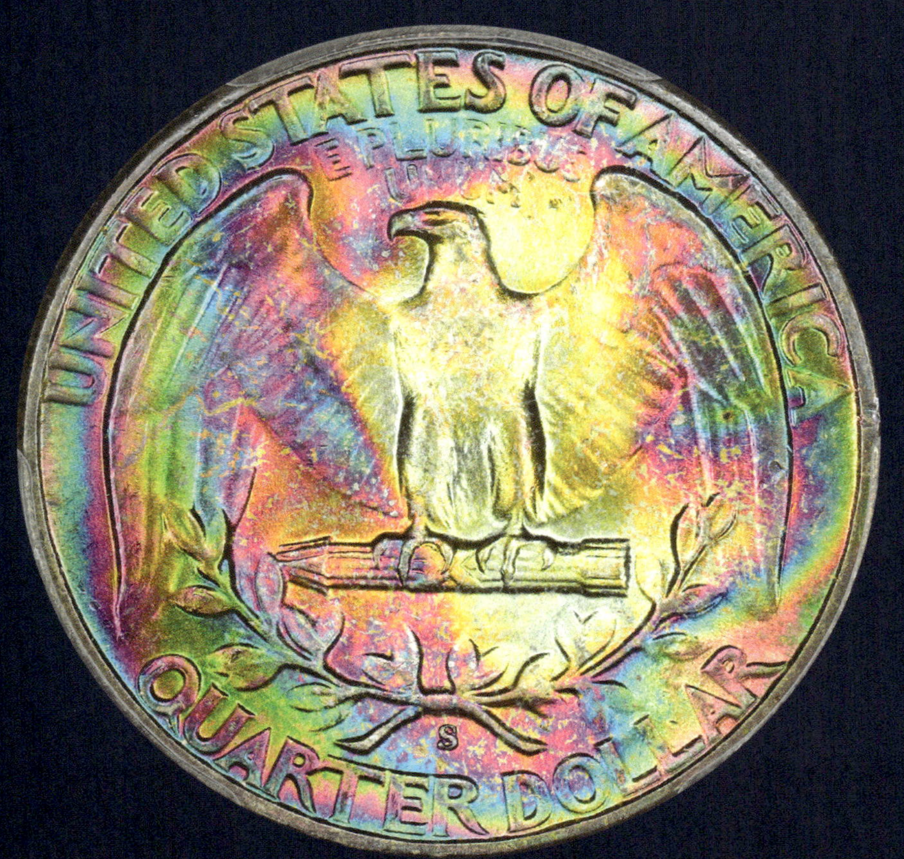

1947-S $.25 PCGS MS64
Certification number 26012461

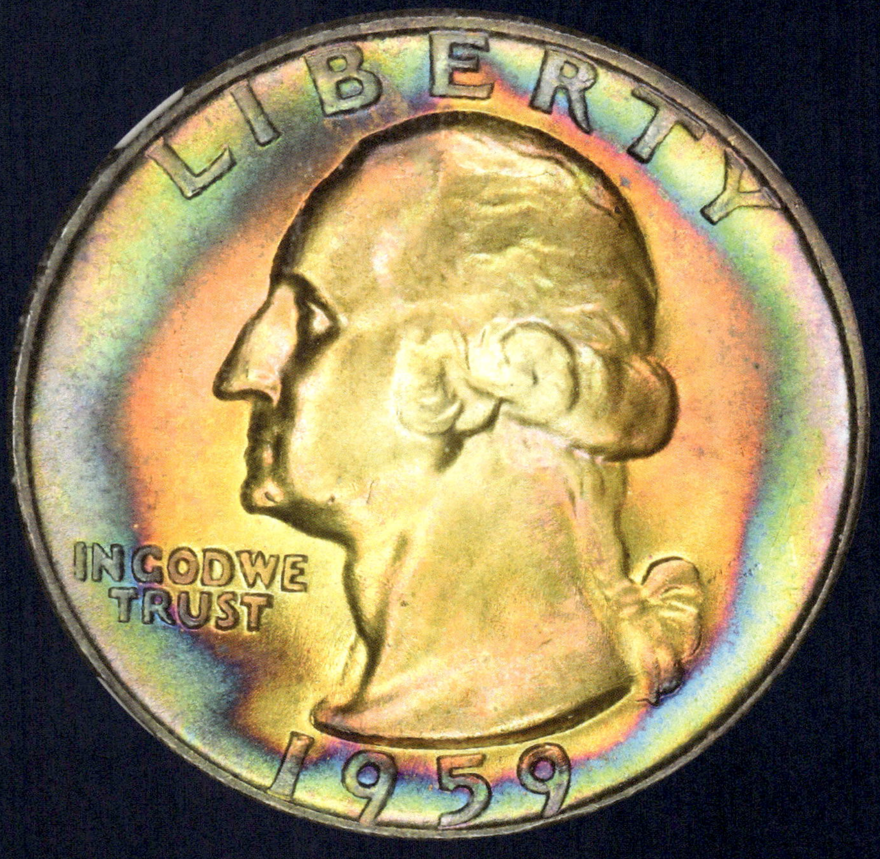

1959-D $.25 NGC MS66
Certification number 4674904-006

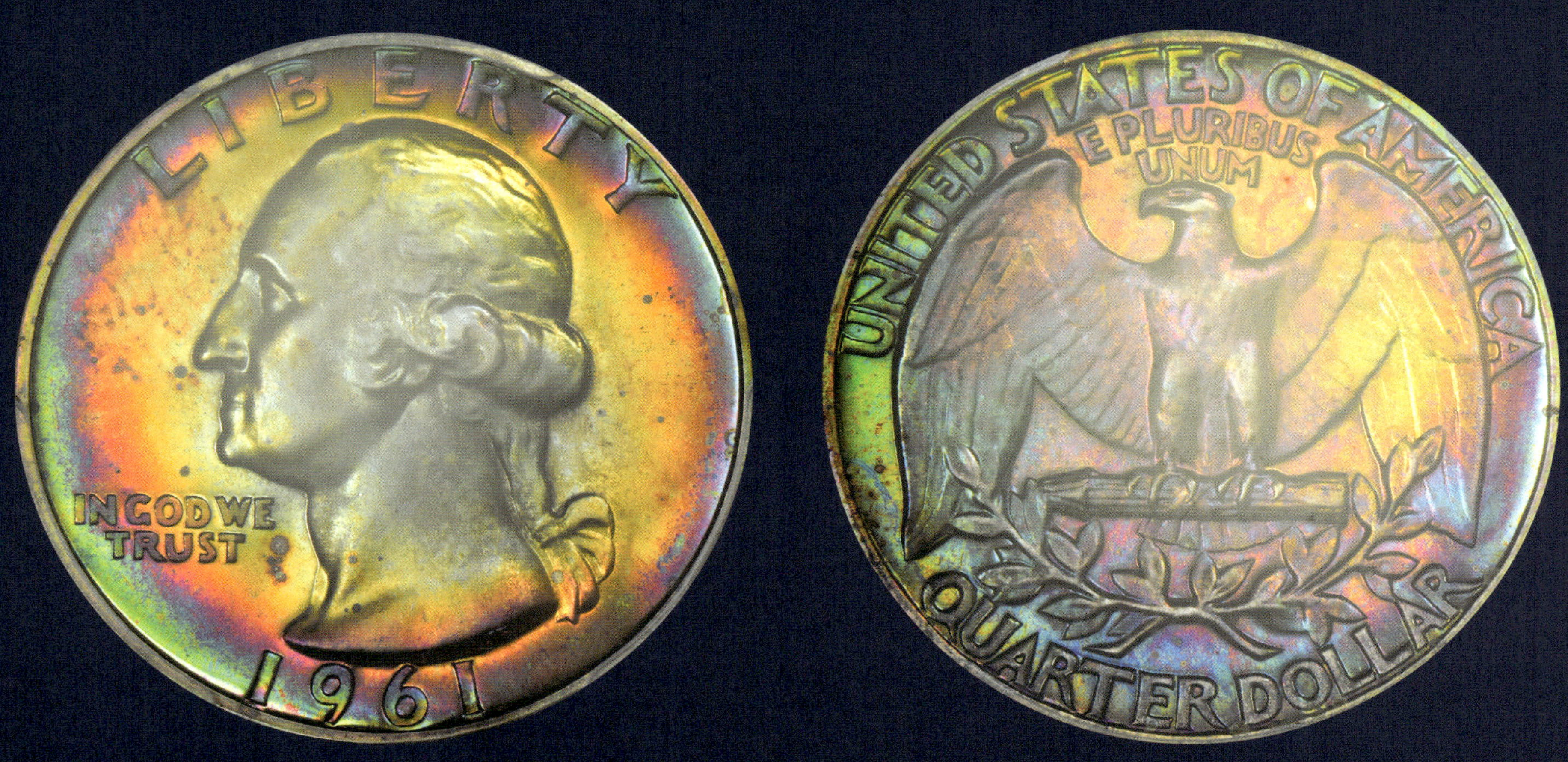

1961 $.25 PCGS PR65
Certification number 37312803

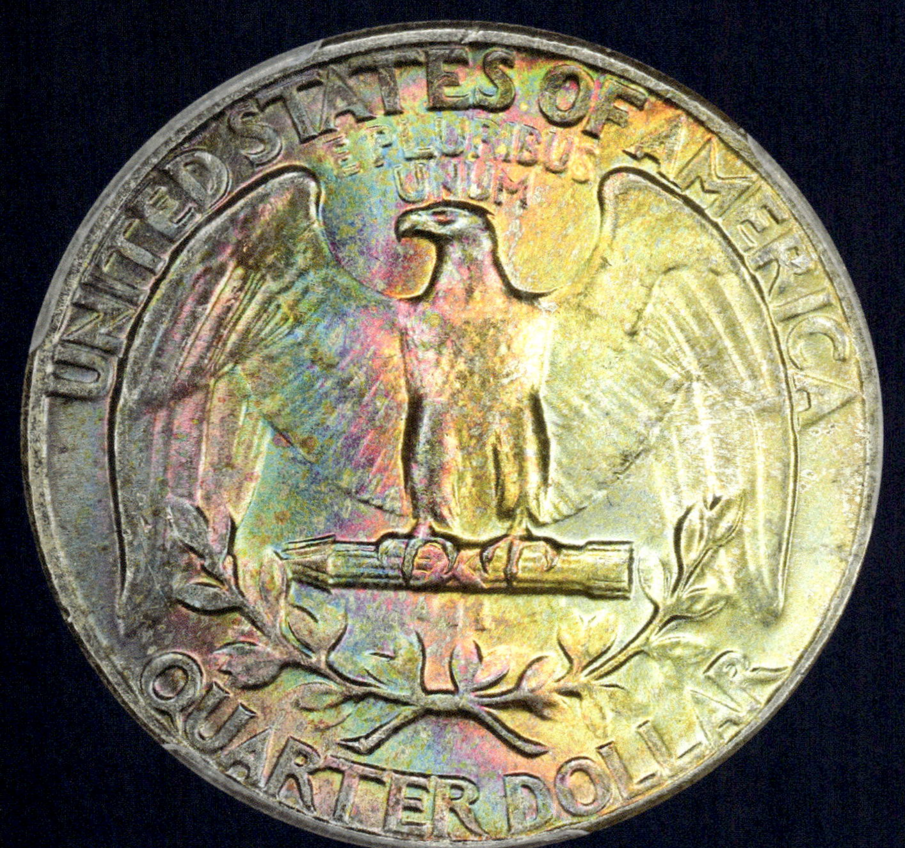

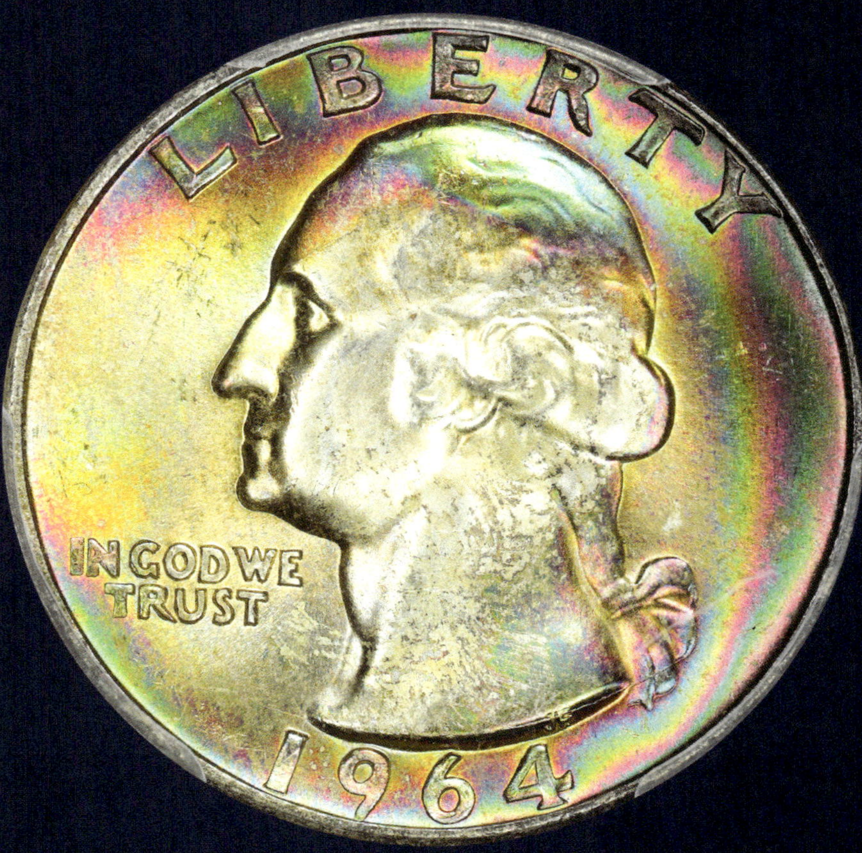

"The Peacock"
1964 $.25 PCGS MS64
Certification number 38410929

1964 $.25 PCGS MS66+
Certification number 37260054

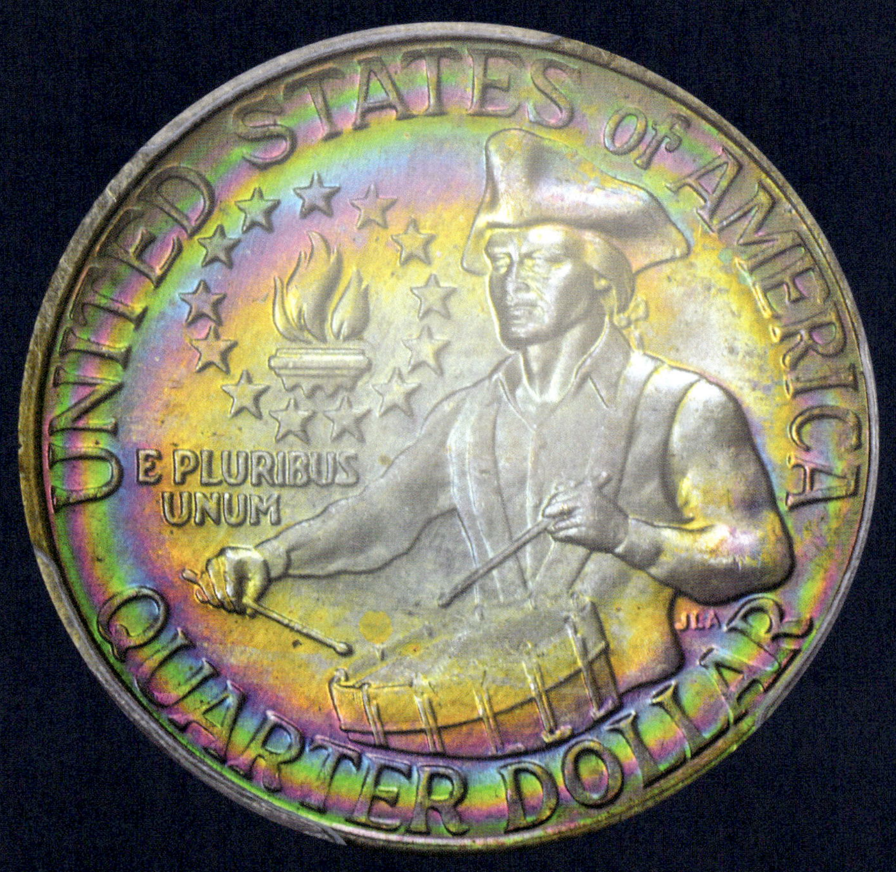

1976 $.25 PCGS MS66 Clad
Certification number 38289419

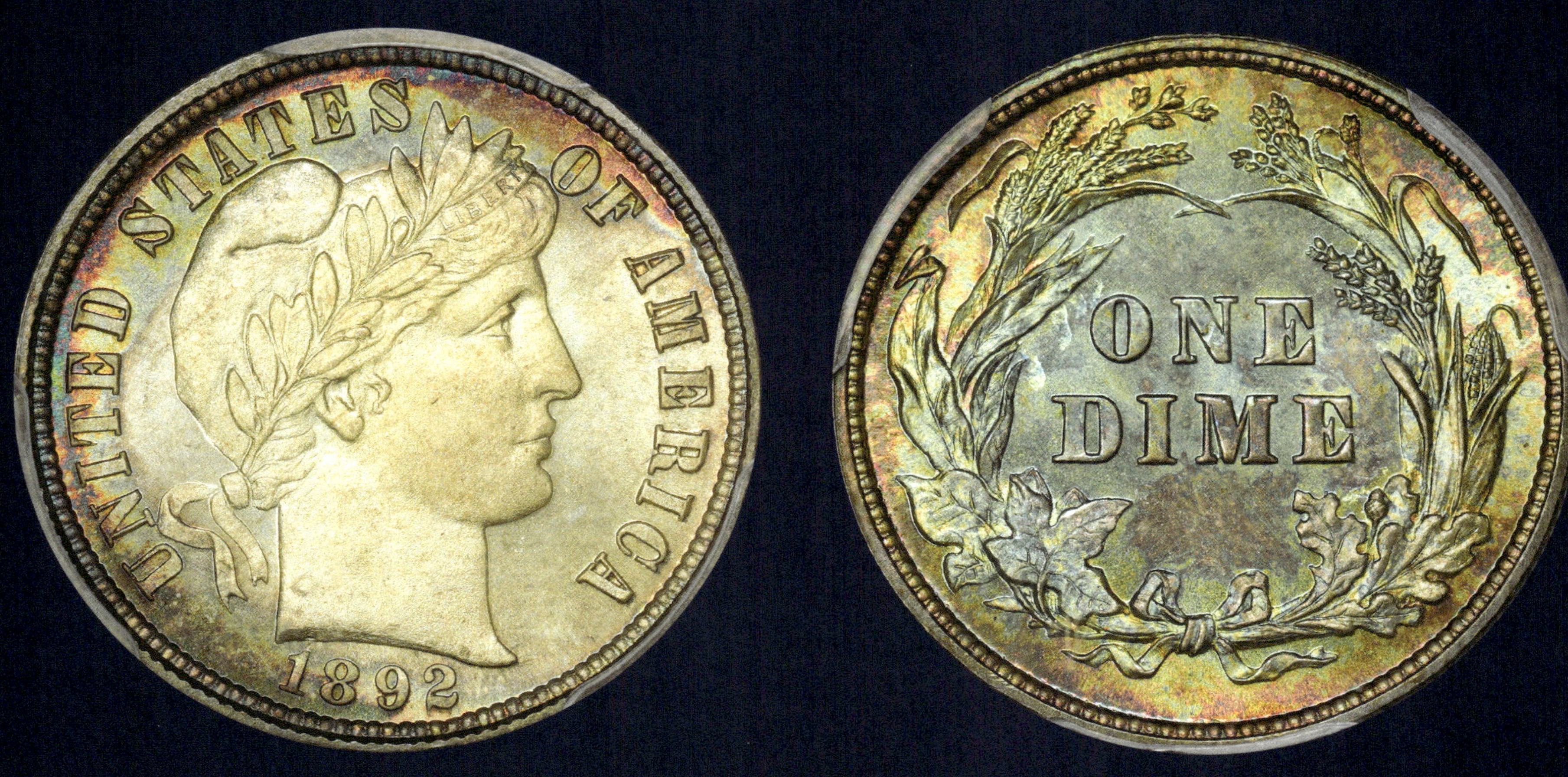

1892 $.10 PCGS MS67+
Certification number 34610293

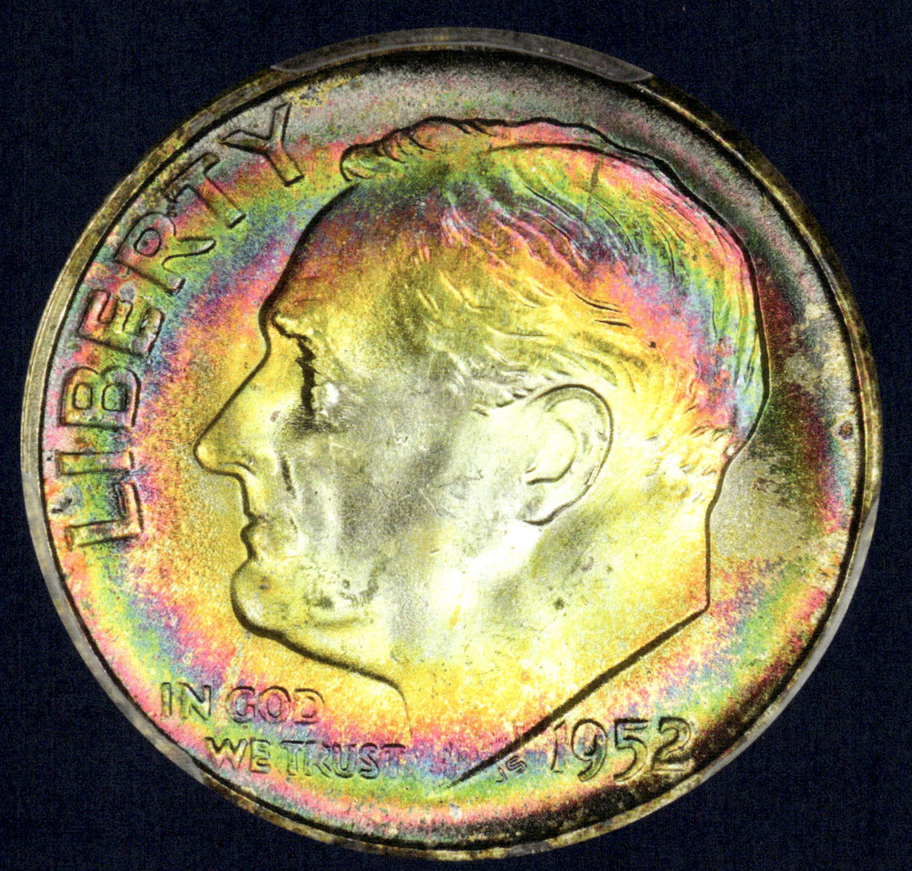

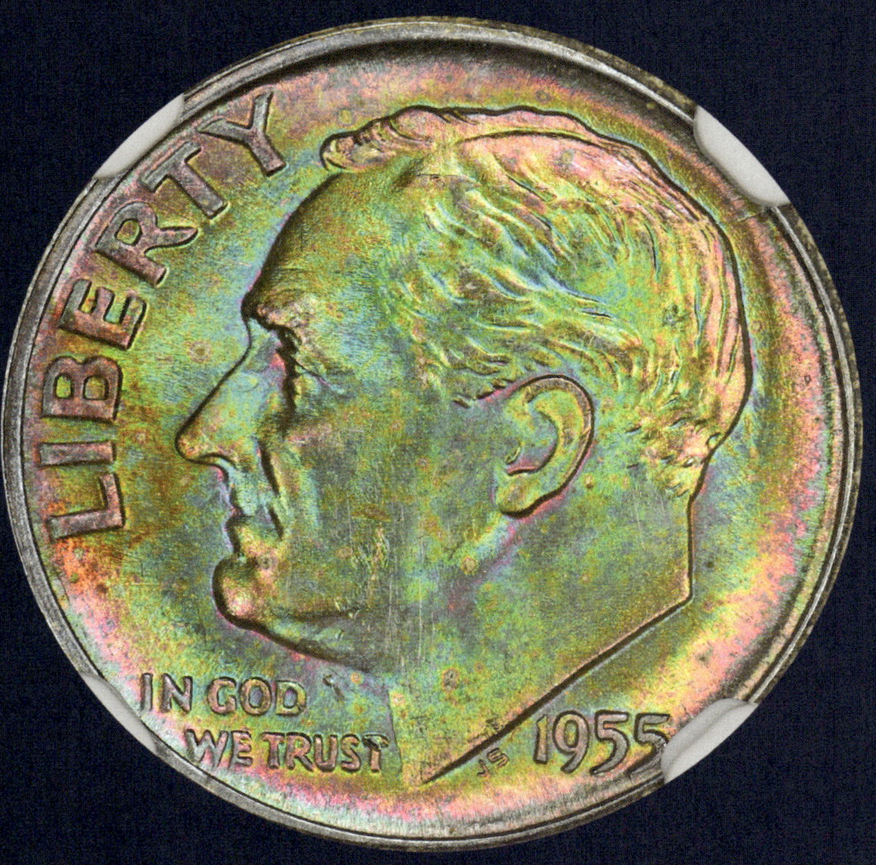

1952-S $.10 PCGS MS67+ FB
Certification number 25799476

1955 $.10 NGC MS66★
Certification number 5709575-001

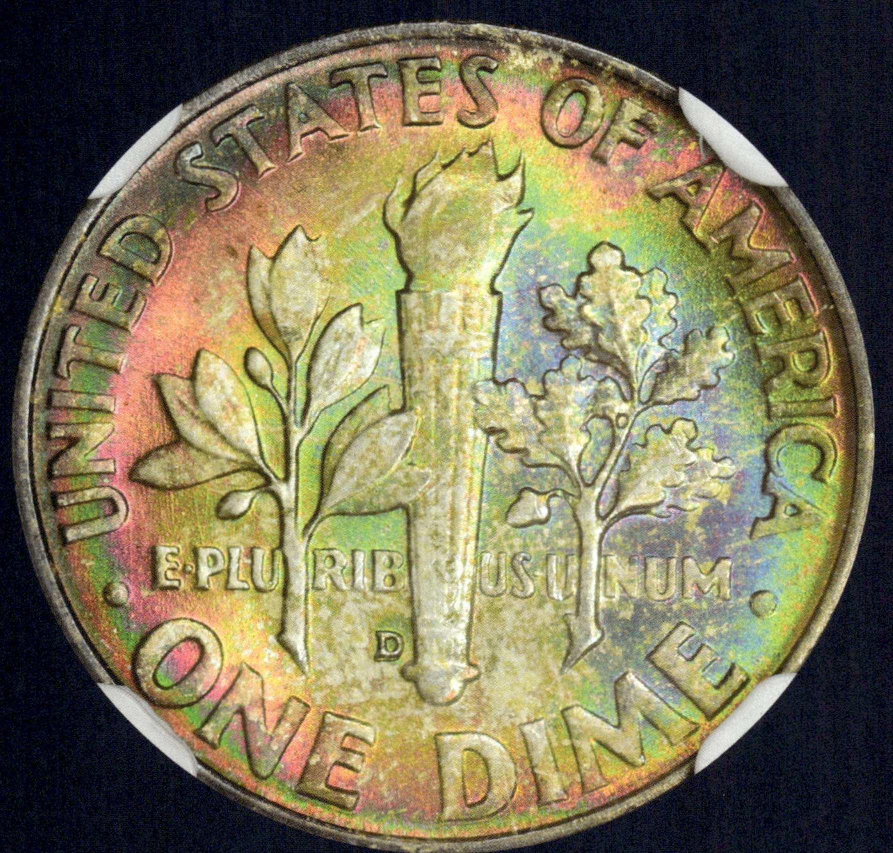

1958-D $.10 NGC MS66
Certification number 4665613-015

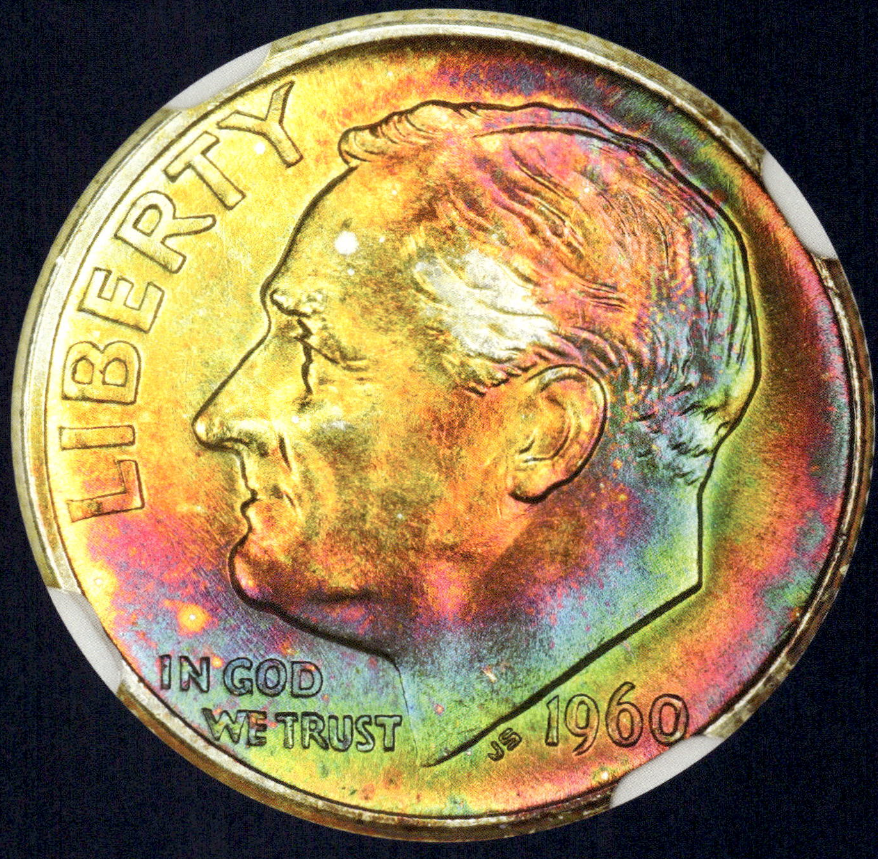

1960-D $.10 NGC MS67★ FT
Certification number 3457692-002

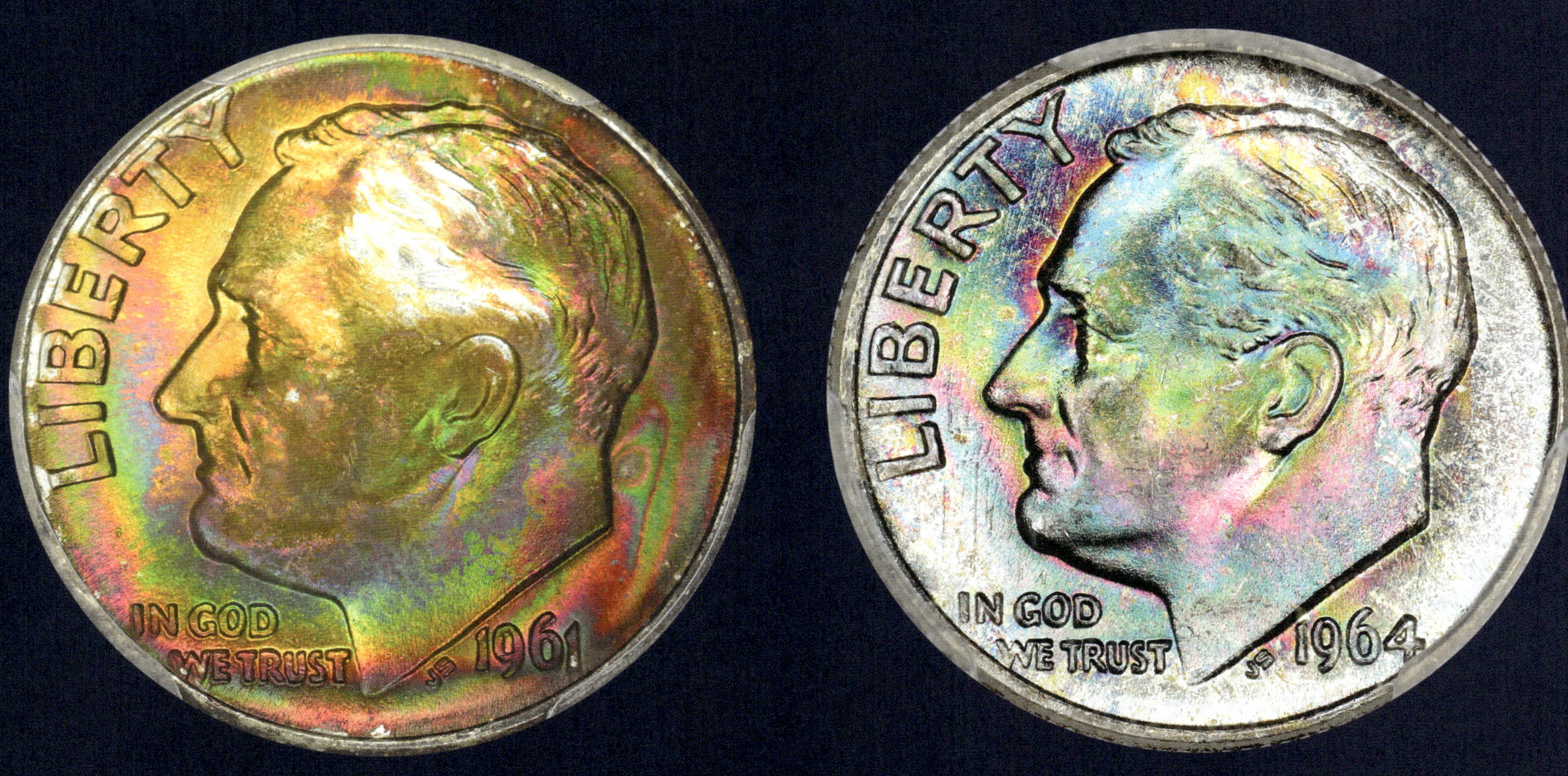

1961-D $.10 PCGS MS67+
Certification number 34488603

1964-D $.10 PCGS MS67+
Certification number 36812778

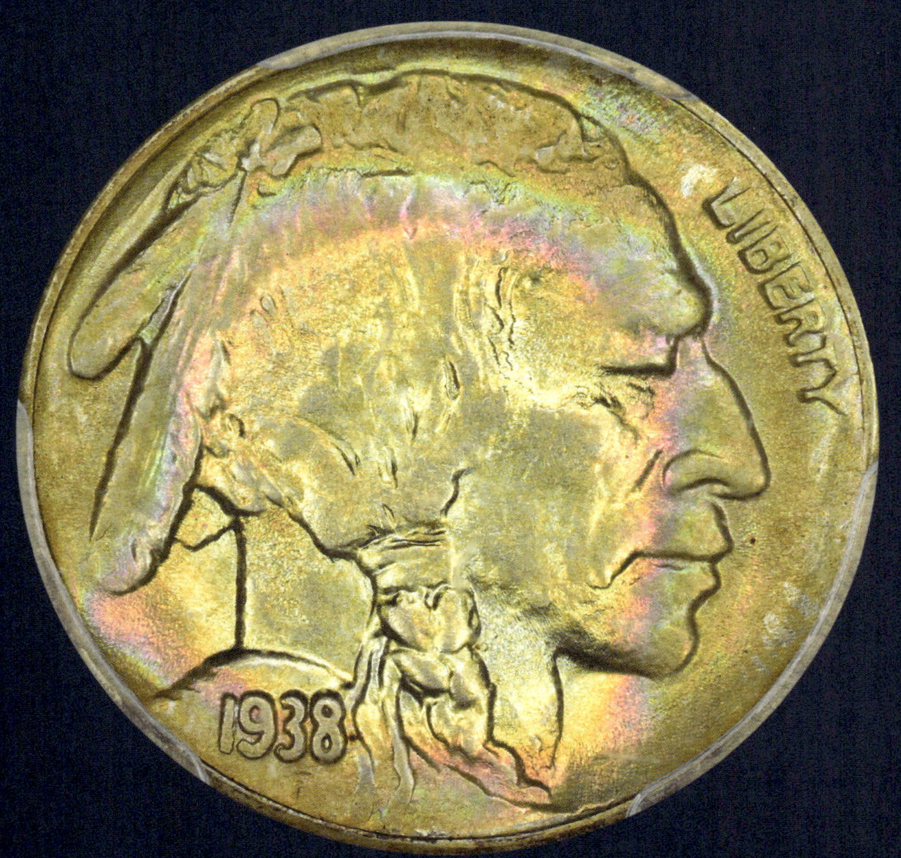

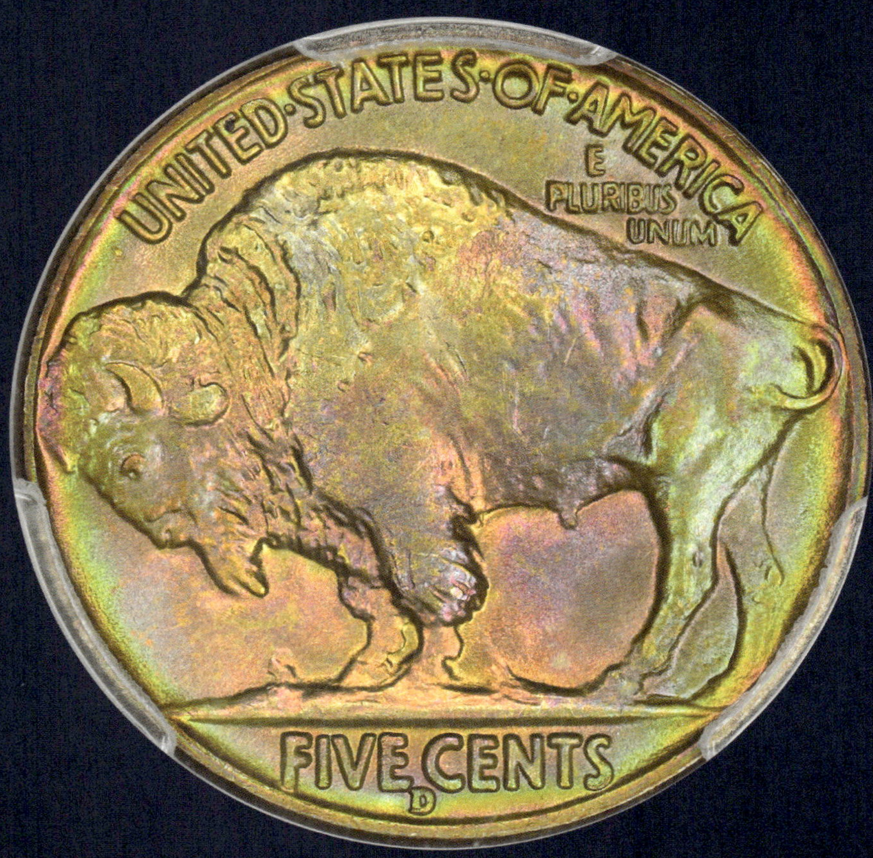

1938-D \$.05 PCGS MS66
Certification number 83897319

1938-D \$.05 PCGS MS66
Certification number 37217438

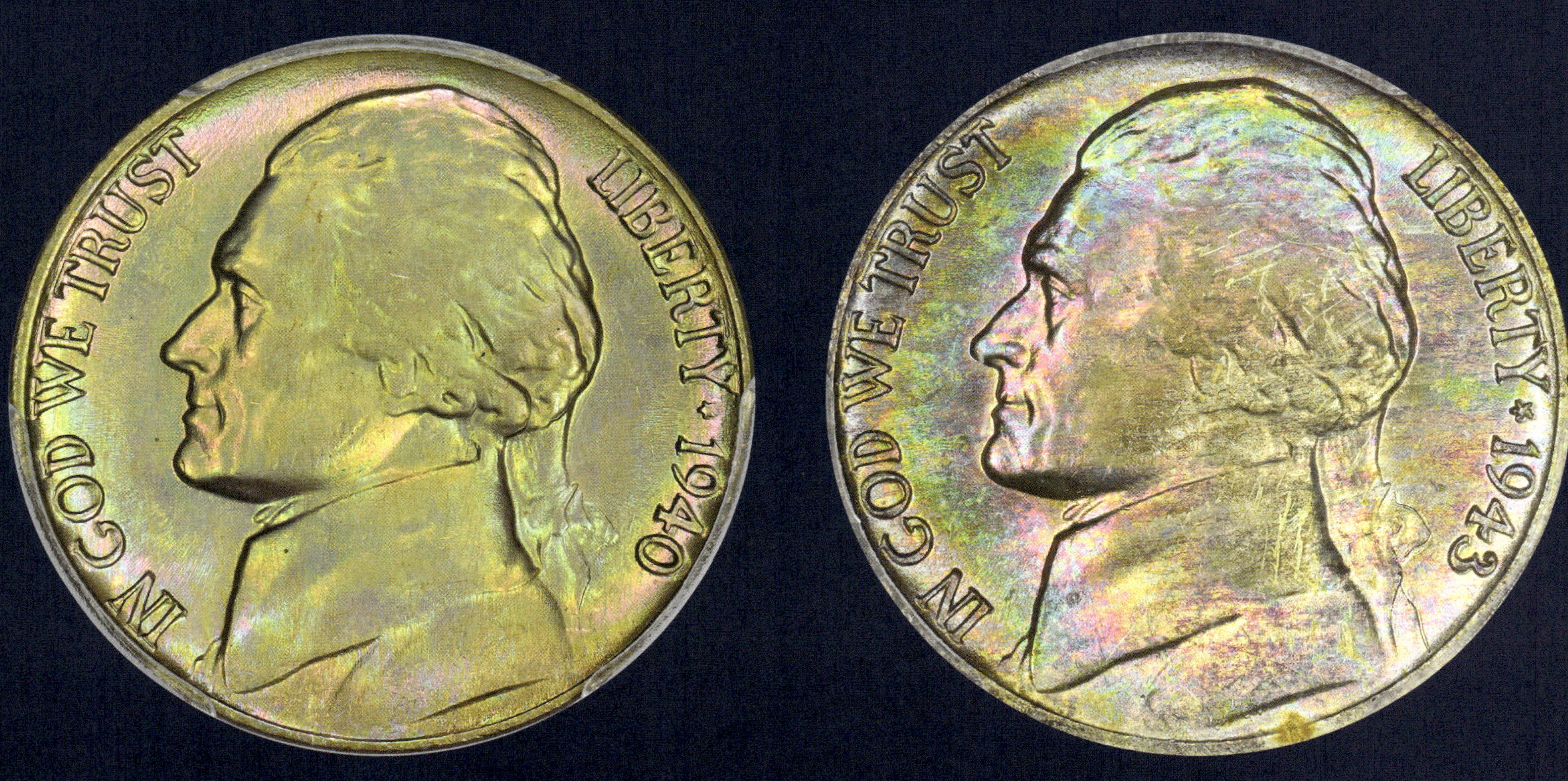

1940 $.05 PCGS MS66
Certification number 36727910

1943 $.05 PCGS MS66
Certification number 34623969

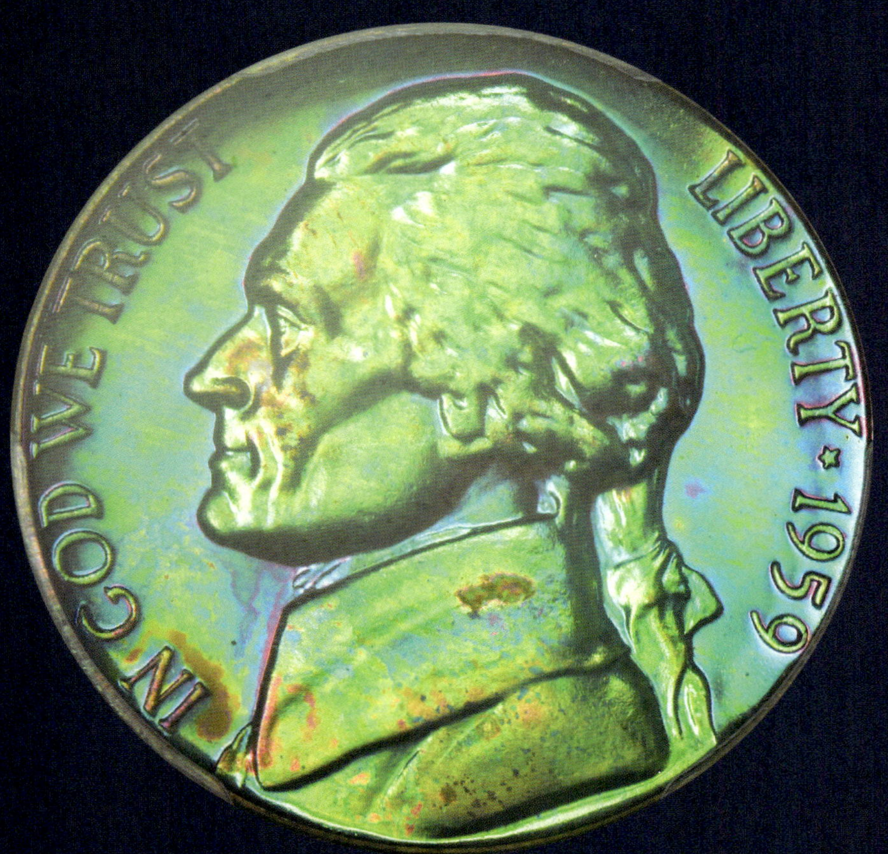

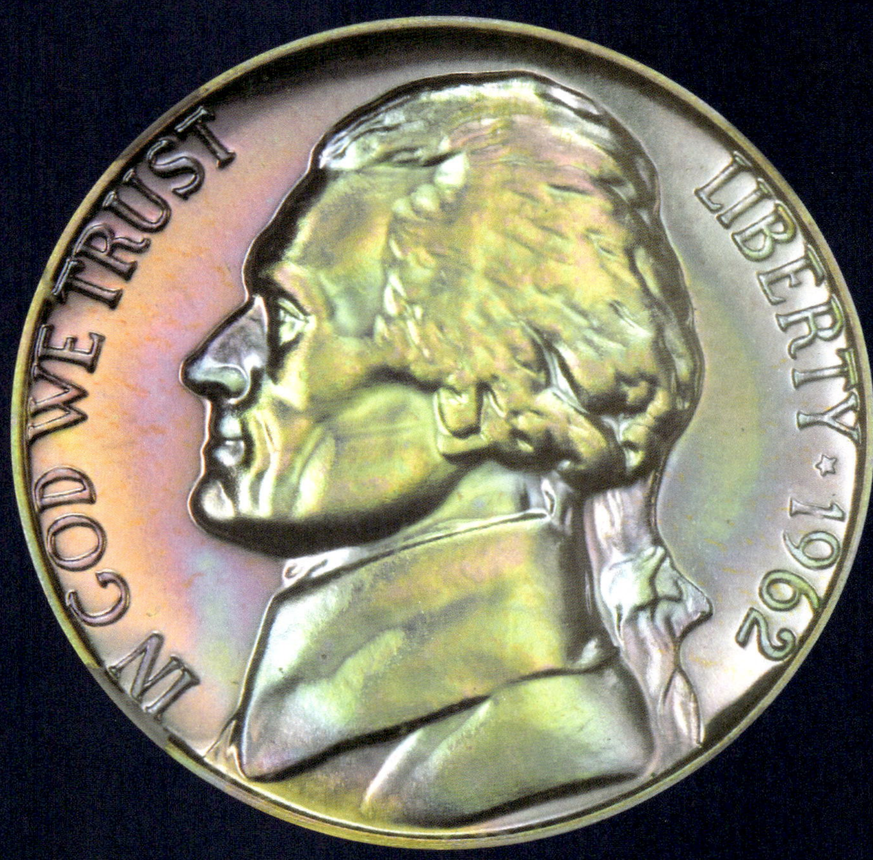

"The Green Light"
1959 $.05 PCGS PR66
Certification number 83440267

"Dreamy Nickel"
1962 $.05 NGC PF67
Certification number 3897146-012

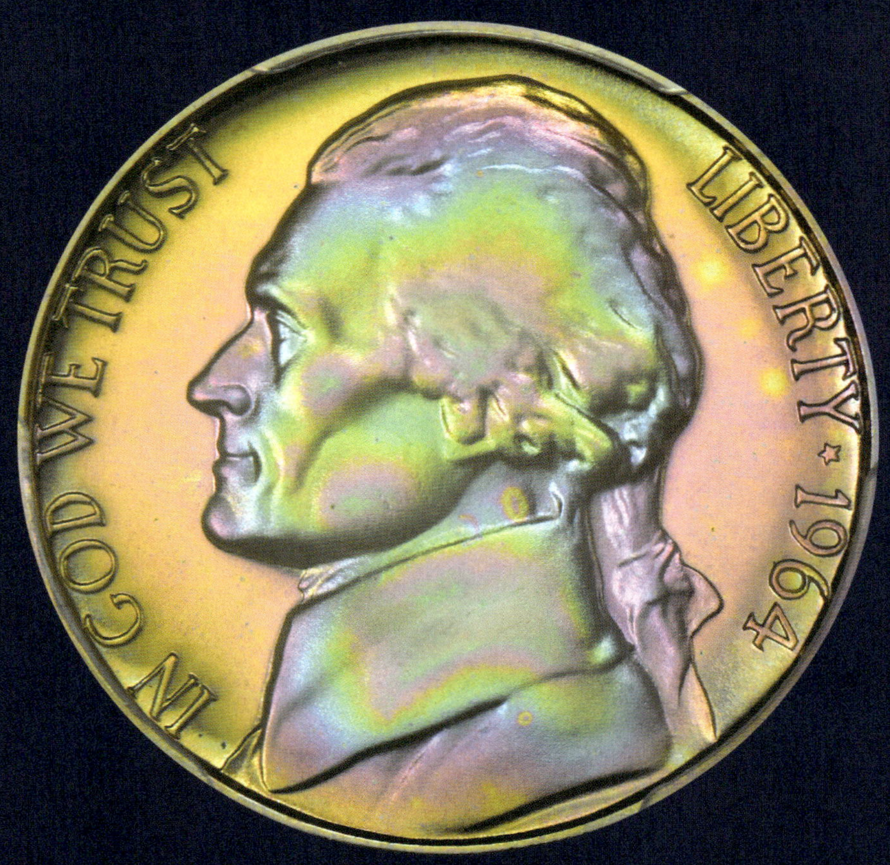

1964 $.05 PCGS PR68
Certification number 32855106

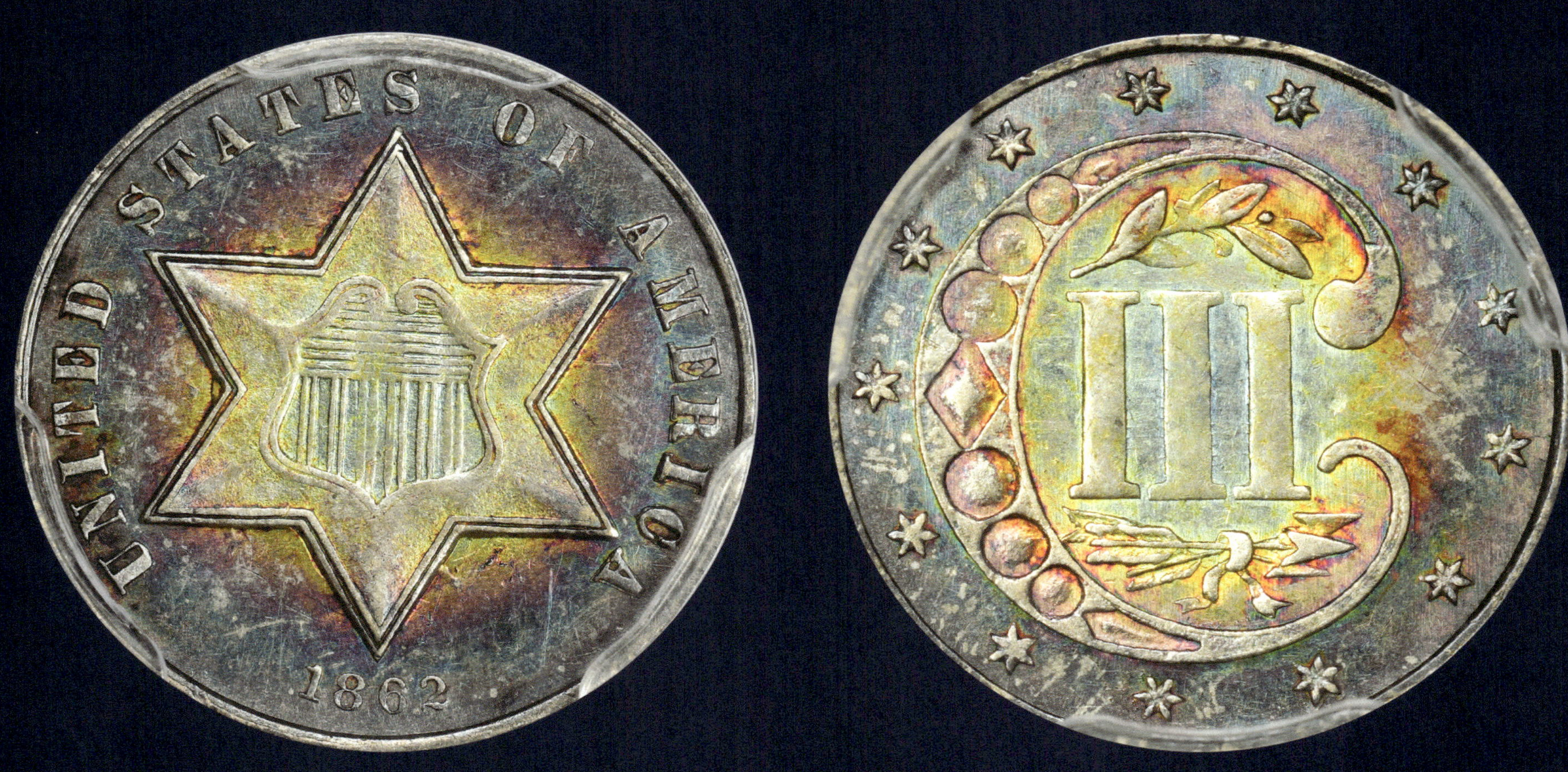

1862 $.03 PCGS MS62
Certification number 84776730

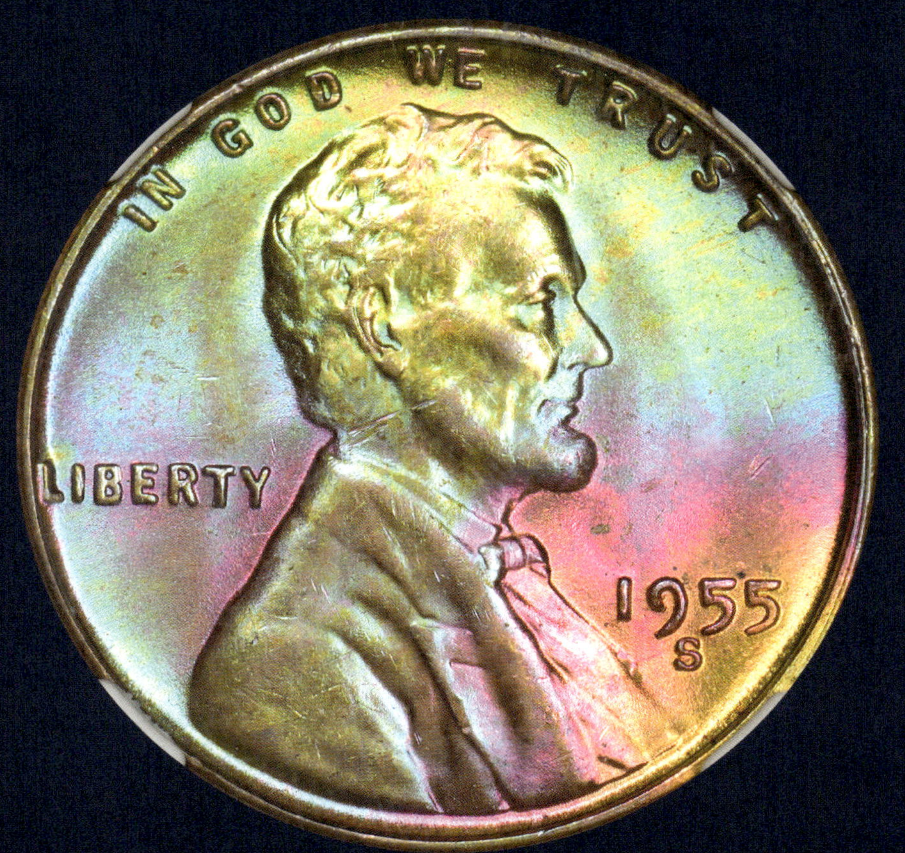

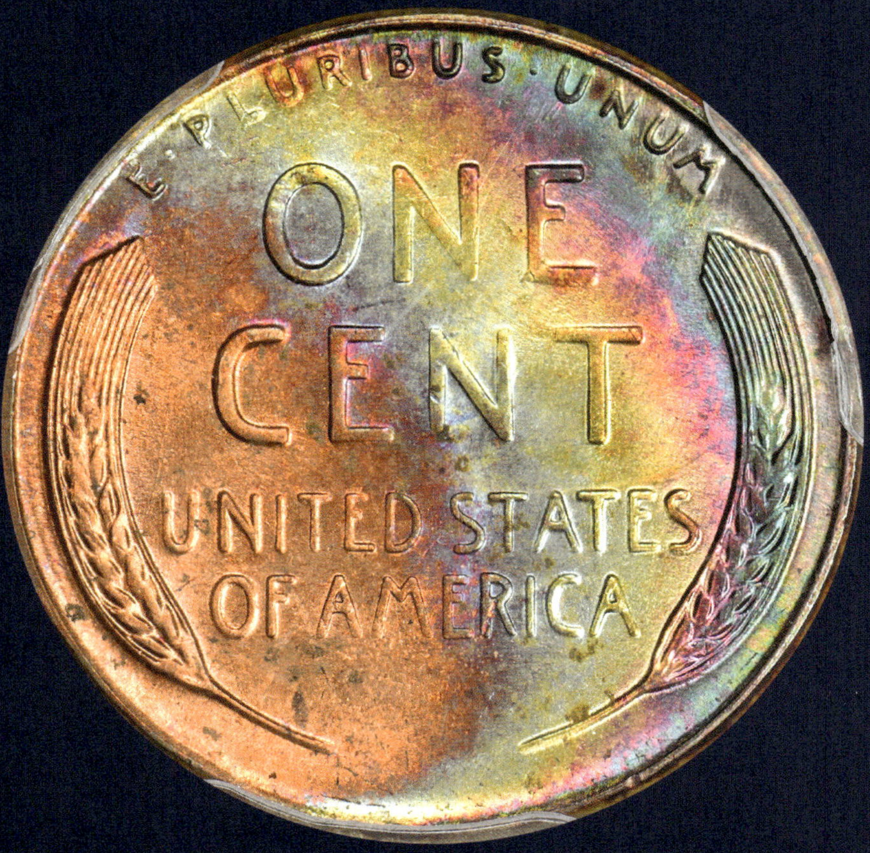

1955-S $.01 NGC MS65RB
Certification number 4739385-005

1958 $.01 PCGS MS65RB
Certification number 85197066

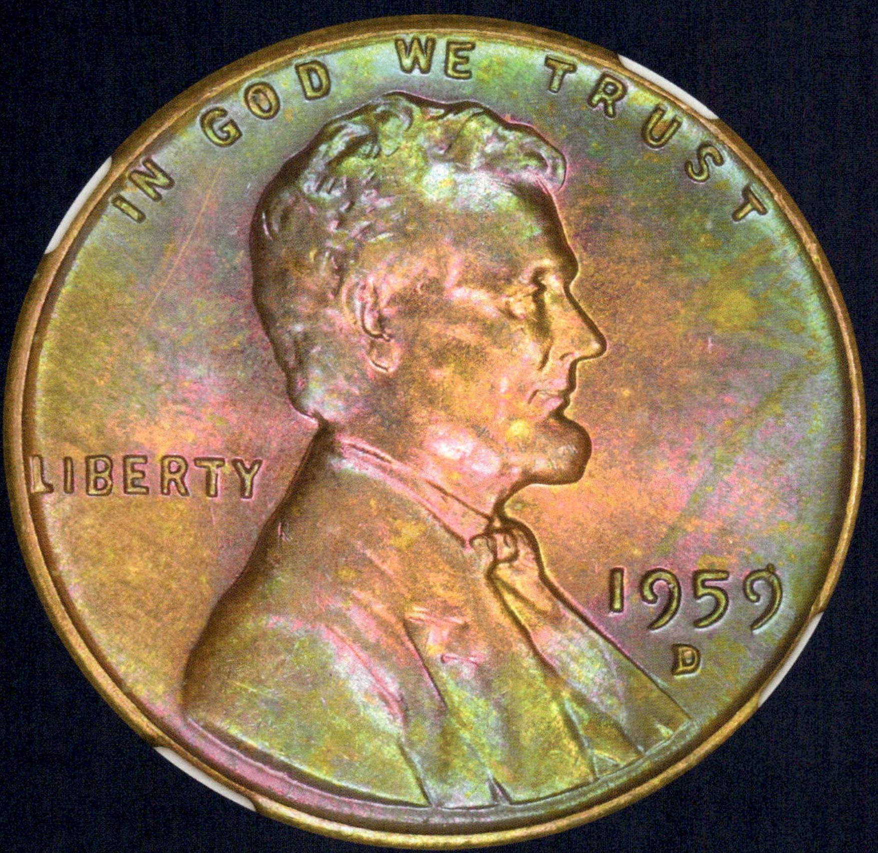

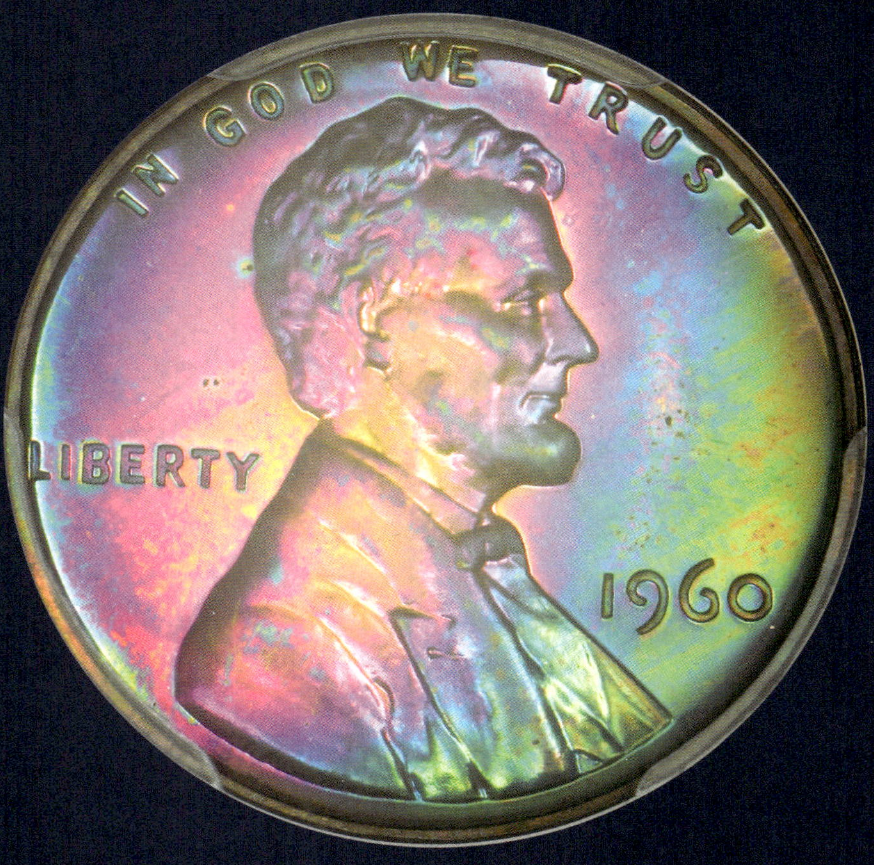

1959-D $.01 NGC MS64BN
Certification number 4829059-006

1960 $.01 PCGS PR66RB Large Date
Certification number 35311513

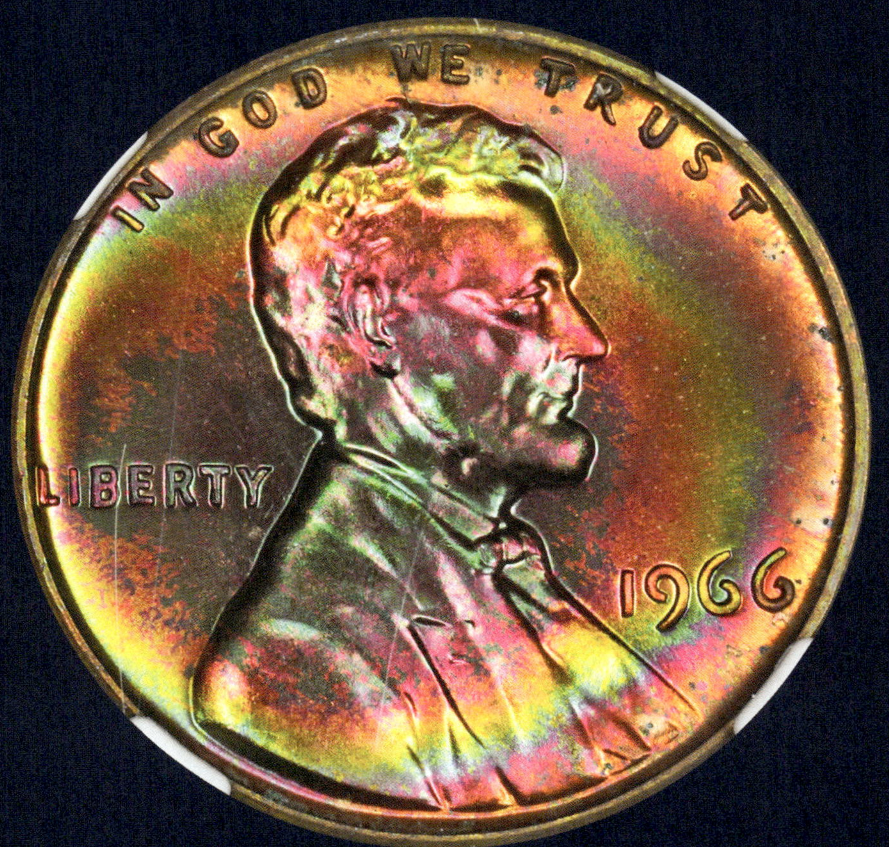

1966 SMS $.01 NGC MS66RB
Certification number 4836597-187

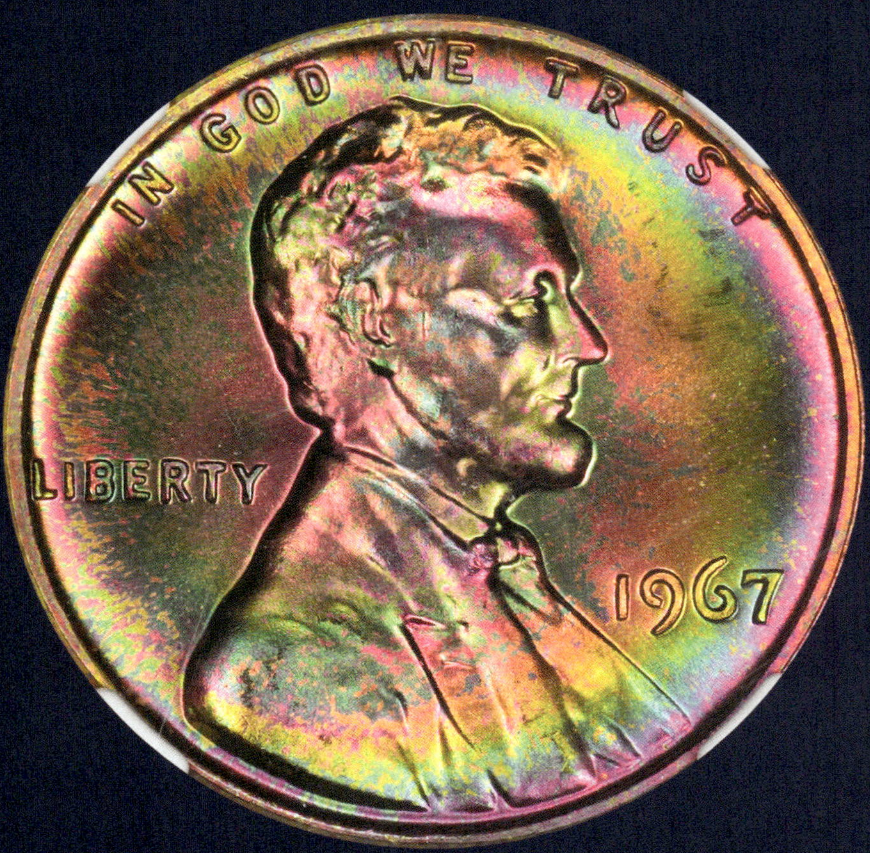

1967 SMS $.01 NGC MS66RB
Certification number 4836597-188

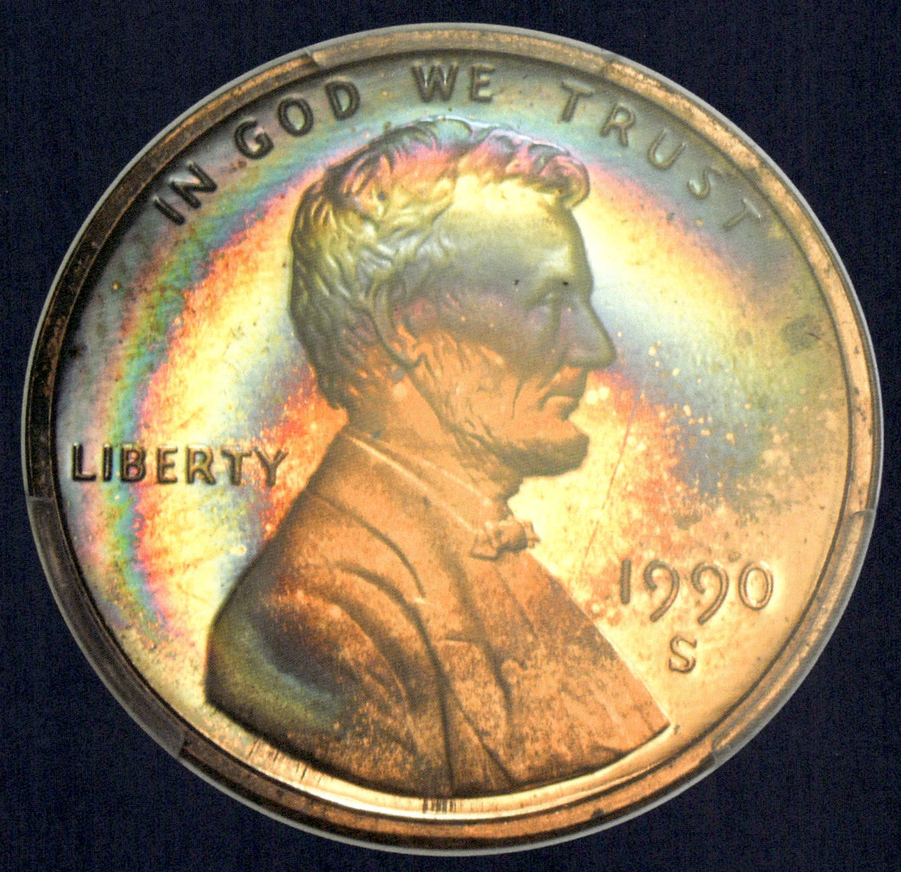

1990-S $.01 PCGS PR66RB
Certification number 38057660

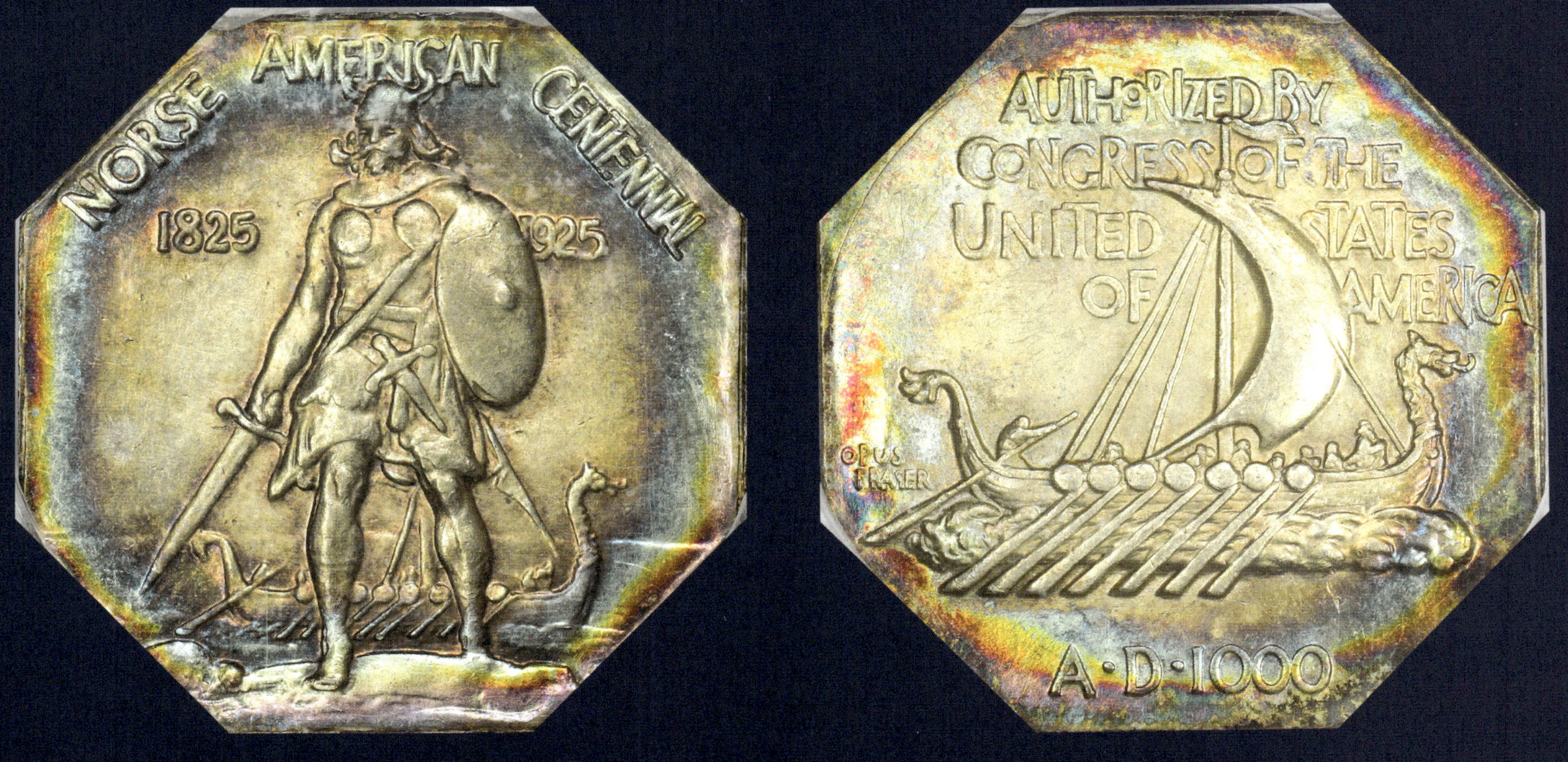

Norse Medal PCGS MS64 Thin
Certification number 35836810